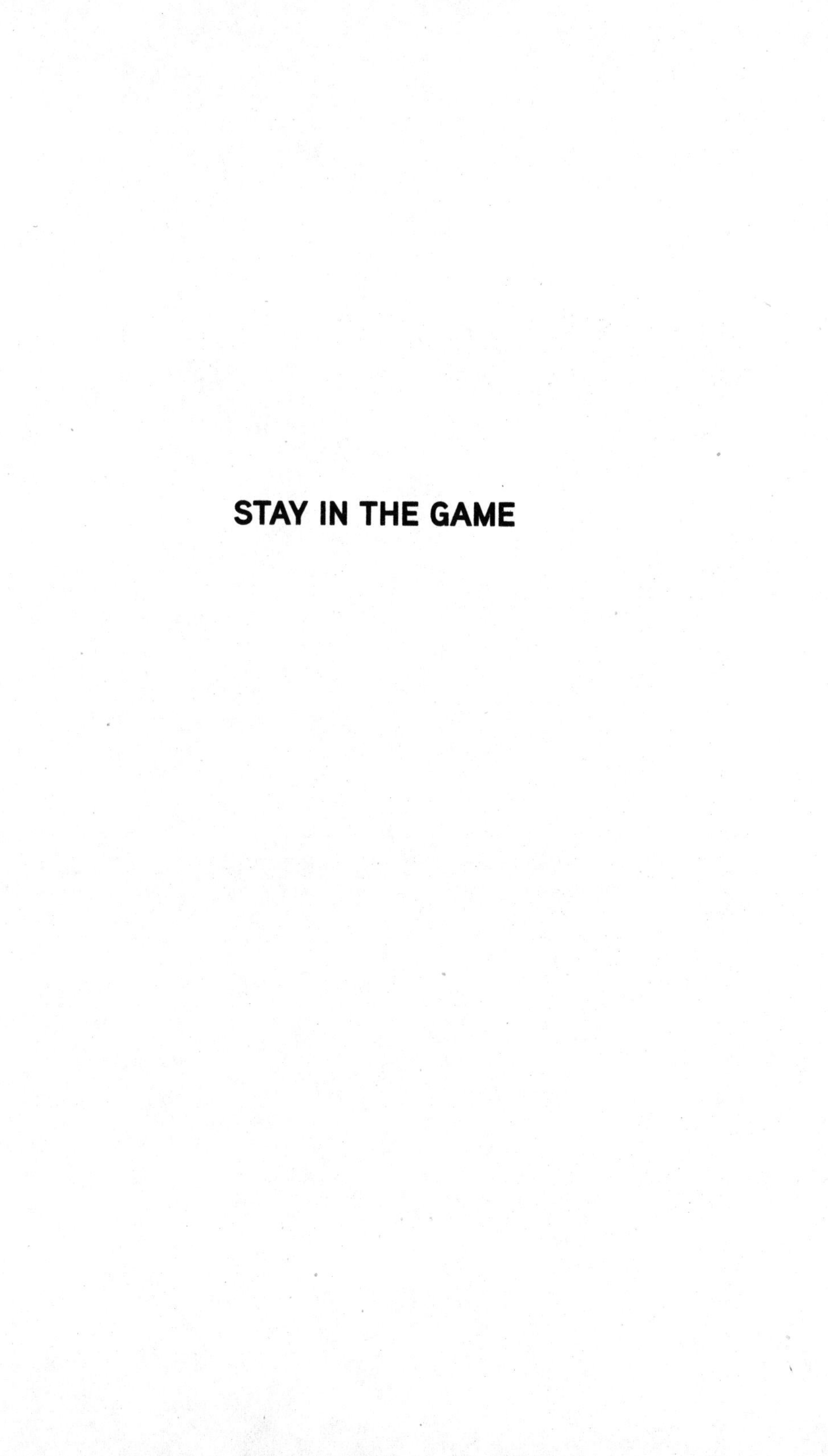

STAY IN THE GAME

MATT FORTÉ

WITH *NEW YORK TIMES* BESTSELLING AUTHOR DAVID L. THOMAS

STAY IN THE GAME

MAKING THE MOST OF EVERY SEASON

A Tyndale nonfiction imprint

Visit Tyndale online at tyndale.com.

Visit Tyndale Momentum online at tyndalemomentum.com.

Tyndale, Tyndale's quill logo, *Tyndale Momentum*, and the Tyndale Momentum logo are registered trademarks of Tyndale House Ministries. Tyndale Momentum is a nonfiction imprint of Tyndale House Publishers, Carol Stream, Illinois.

Stay in the Game: Making the Most of Every Season

Cover design by Alberto C. Navata Jr.

Interior design by Cathy Miller

For information about special discounts for bulk purchases, please contact Tyndale House Publishers at csresponse@tyndale.com, or call 1-855-277-9400.

Library of Congress Cataloging-in-Publication Data

A catalog record for this book is available from the Library of Congress.

ISBN 979-8-4005-1078-6

Printed in the United States of America

31 30 29 28 27 26 25
7 6 5 4 3 2 1

Contents

Foreword

I'll never forget the first time I met Matt Forté in person. First impressions matter.

I was entering my fifth season as head coach of the Chicago Bears and nearing my third decade as a coach. We had selected Matt in the second round of the 2008 NFL draft, and he and the other rookies were reporting to their first meeting at Halas Hall, the Bears' headquarters.

Matt walked in wearing a suit. I had never seen a new player report to a team in coat and tie, and I never saw it again through the rest of my coaching career. Every other player showed up in sweatpants, sweatshirts, shorts, or T-shirts. Matt was different. He was there to play football, just like his peers, but he also was on a business trip. He viewed his first official day with the Bears as the most important job interview of his life, and he treated it as such.

That day, Matt set the tone—not only for the first day of his rookie season but also for his entire career. Matt was a professional in every sense of the word.

Now that I'm retired from football, I enjoy looking back on the big games and moments that occurred during my five decades in the sport. But I most relish the opportunity to reflect on the relationships I developed through football, especially with the hundreds of players I was blessed to coach. In a tough sport like football, in a job packed with pressure to win, a coach can't afford to play favorites. But every coach has his favorite players. Mine were those who went about the sport and business of football the right way, and who I knew would give everything they had to the coaching staff and their teammates, 24/7.

Matt Forté was one of my favorite players.

Matt asking me to write the foreword for his book is one of the great honors I have received from one of my former players. I had to chuckle as I thought about the stories I could tell about Matt, because compared to the stories I could tell about other players I coached, some might say my stories about Matt were boring. And that's a compliment to Matt!

The best surprise for an NFL head coach is to not have any surprises. We want our players to be who we believe they are, in every circumstance, and that's precisely who Matt is.

We drafted Matt with the forty-fourth overall pick. Our top need entering the 2008 draft was an offensive lineman, and we filled that need by selecting Chris Williams in the first round. We had also identified "running back" as another crucial need. During our draft preparation, running backs coach Tim Spencer told me that Matt was the running back we wanted. Other running backs were ranked higher than Matt, I guess in part because he came from Tulane University, which was not a powerhouse football program.

But when we watched Matt's film from Tulane, he clearly had all the skills necessary to be a top back in the NFL. He had the speed to go the distance, could catch the ball well, and was a good blocker. In Chicago, a running back has to be big enough and tough enough to run between the tackles and play in bad weather. Matt checked those boxes too. And he was intelligent.

Though the draft was deep at running back, we didn't know if Matt would last until our pick early in the second round. Five running backs were taken in the first round, but Matt was still on the board when our turn came again. We were delighted to select him.

Matt arrived in Chicago wearing a nice suit and a chip on his shoulder. I'm sure he felt disrespected after seeing five other backs drafted ahead of him. Our team and Bears fans benefited from Matt's drive to prove the other teams wrong.

Everything we saw in Matt on film showed up on the practice field. All we had learned about him off the field was also evident. He immediately showed himself to be coachable and a student of the game. He quickly picked up our offense—not an easy task for a rookie running back. He was never late for a meeting. He respected and listened to our veteran leaders.

Rookie running backs taken high in the draft usually arrive with enough talent to start for their team. But many don't start right away, because it takes time to learn everything about a complex NFL offense. That was not the case with Matt, and I was able to call him into my office before the first game of the regular season and tell him that he would begin the season as our starting running back.

Matt took great pride in not just starting but in being an every-down back. Even good, veteran NFL running backs encounter issues with catching the ball and pass protection. Again, not Matt. Because of his intelligence, work ethic, determination, and the natural gifts the Lord blessed him with, he was as good a receiver out of the backfield as he was a running back taking a handoff from the quarterback. He also had our coaching staff's complete trust to stay on the field for pass protection.

I was Matt's head coach for his first five years in the league. We had veteran leadership in our locker room and a strong faith presence, which allowed Matt to come in as a rookie and simply fit in. But being the starting running back for the Bears—the same role on the same franchise that Walter Payton fulfilled as well as any back in NFL history—also carried public responsibilities. The TV reporters' microphones and print media's recorders were part of the landscape around Matt's locker. Let me tell you, there are some players in the league that coaches don't want speaking into a microphone. Or who at least need to be coached up on how to speak to the media. Again, not Matt. Even though he's a rather quiet guy, Matt understood the importance of representing our team—and our city—to the media. As head coach, I *wanted* Matt to speak on behalf of our team. He boosted our brand.

Matt also embraced the city of Chicago and the opportunity to be a role model. I grew up playing football in Texas, and I'm proud of my East Texas roots. But there is no greater city than Chicago. The Bears mean everything in Chicago. To his credit, Matt, a southern Louisiana boy, moved to Chicago and became a leader in our community. He still lives there, and he has only expanded his involvement, post-retirement, in making some of the city's roughest areas safer and better places to live, work, and play. I have three sons who grew up following the teams I coached. I wanted them to see Matt, hear Matt, and be around Matt. I have twelve grandchildren now. Matt is the type of role model I hope they will find too.

Finally, my favorite aspect of my relationship with Matt is that I can call him a brother in Christ. The NFL life appears glamorous to outsiders, but I assure you it is far from that. Once a player becomes publicly recognizable, temptations are everywhere. In Matt's case, he had the added attention that comes with being a young, attractive running back for the Chicago Bears. I appreciate how Matt is open in this book about his faith and the struggles that came with his celebrity. His honesty is refreshing in today's image-protecting culture, and I know he shares his experiences and mistakes so that others can learn from them. Matt learned and grew as a man. And he never allowed anything to affect who he wanted to be as a football player and teammate.

From the first time I met him—standing out because of his suit—Matt Forté has always taken care of business.

Lovie Smith
Chicago Bears head coach, 2004–2012

Prologue

Ball cradled in my right arm, I turn the corner, dipping my left shoulder ever so slightly to create momentum as I step out of my cut. Squaring my shoulders, I reach full speed by my second step. I lock my eyes on the defender heading toward me. With my speed, I think he'll either miss the tackle or I'll break through his arms and stay on my feet. Either way, I'm not slowing down.

The next thing I know, I'm flat on my back, looking up at the hot Louisiana sun. I remain on the ground, taking inventory of my body parts as the feeling slowly returns to my extremities.

That hurt a little bit.

Water begins pooling in my eyes. Then tears start sliding down my cheeks. I look to the side as the large shadow of a man eclipses the sun.

It's my dad, one of my coaches.

He stoops over until he's close to my face mask, and he says matter-of-factly, "That's football, Son."

I'm seven years old, at my first football practice, and that was my very first carry—my introduction to the sport I had begged to play, even though my dad, a man with eight-inch scars on the insides of both knees from his own playing days, had told me I should wait a year.

And now he's telling me, "That's football, Son."

The human brain is an amazing creation—able to process a rush of thoughts in mere seconds, and able to rationalize even at a young age. At that moment, I realize not only that football is a physical sport but also how I need to respond to having been planted into the grass of a city park practice field.

With those tears still finding their way down my face, I look squarely up at my dad, bite hard on my mouthpiece, and grunt my reply.

"I wanna go again."

I roll over to my right—realizing for the first time that I hadn't fumbled!—spring to my feet, and head straight to the front of the line of kids waiting their turn to carry the ball in the drill.

The coaches tell the same defender to step in to take me on again.

It's him or me, I tell myself. *And it's not gonna be me.*

When the coach blows his whistle, I take the same first step, make the same turn to the left, and accelerate to full speed. I see the same would-be-tackler heading straight toward me with the same bad intentions. But this time I have the benefit of a lesson learned. Instead of running high—standing too tall and making myself a target—I lower my left shoulder, determined to *deliver* the hit rather than absorb it.

You don't need to have played football to understand what happened next. Athletes in other sports will know what I mean. It's like a golfer or a baseball player who strikes the ball so purely, so perfectly, that they don't feel the contact. Instead, it's as if the ball *jumps* off the clubface or bat, the uninterrupted motion through impact making their swing look effortless. That's the best way I can describe my second career carry in football. I hear the *pop!* when our shoulder pads collide, but I run right through the defender like he was never there and continue sprinting into the wide-open field ahead of me.

As I turn and jog back to the rest of the team, I'm not thinking about the teammate I left on the ground behind me. I wasn't seeking revenge against him. I'm not looking to see what my coaches and teammates have to say about my run. I wasn't trying to redeem myself.

Instead, I'm thinking, *I know I can do this if I do it the right way.*

That thought, that feeling, is immensely gratifying. I have discovered the spark—the fuel—for my desire to play football, for the confidence that I can play this game, especially as a running back. If "that's football," as my dad told me, I love it and I want to keep playing.

After that first practice, I loaded my gear into my dad's car and hopped into the passenger seat. Before he could say anything or ask me a question, I wanted to make a statement, with full conviction in my heart and in my voice: "I'm going to be a professional football player when I grow up."

I can still hear my dad's voice whenever I think of that defining moment in my young life.

"That's football, Son."

Football is a tough sport. Football players are tough because the game demands it of us. We must choose to be tough to stay in the game, because football is tough by design.

The average length of an NFL career is 3.3 seasons. For running backs—my position—the average is only 2.67. That's why many who have played at football's highest level say that NFL stands for "Not For Long."

By playing ten seasons in the pros, I crushed the odds.

The mindset that allowed me to not just *play* all those seasons but also stay on the field as an every-down back for the better part of my career, started when I was seven years old, in a city park in Slidell, Louisiana. The day I received the jarring introduction to the sport I would play for the next twenty-five years, my dad told me precisely what I needed to hear. He didn't try to console me when I got knocked down. He didn't try to stroke my ego when I had success. He wasn't even trying to challenge me. True to his nature, my dad told me the plain truth. He has always had the ability to communicate a lot of truth in very few words. And the message packed inside those three little words he spoke as he leaned over me that day was, *You say you want to play football. I support you. But you need to know that* this *is what you signed up for.*

My dad looked a little surprised when I told him I was ready to give it another try. I might have seen a little pride on his face too—as if he was happy to discover that his youngest son had some dog in him.

From that day forward, I never doubted football would be tough. Or that I would need to be tougher than the sport.

Every down.

Every game.

Every season.

1

GROWING UP A FORTÉ

"Play for the name on the front of your jersey" is a common way of telling athletes to prioritize the team over individual accomplishments. I played football with a team-first mindset while proudly wearing the jerseys of the Slidell High Tigers, the Tulane Green Wave, the Chicago Bears, and the New York Jets.

I also understood the responsibility that came with having *FORTE* stitched across the back of my shoulders. The generations of Fortés who came before me saw to it that our family name would stand for characteristics like integrity, hard work, excellence, and always giving your best regardless of circumstances.

More than anyone else, my parents, Gene and Gilda Forté, made me both the athlete and man I've become. I am eternally grateful for how they raised me, inconspicuously making sacrifices for my brother, Bryan, and me, bringing us up with a foundation of faith, teaching us the value of hard work, and instilling discipline into our character.

I was born in Lake Charles, Louisiana, on December 10, 1985. Lake Charles is less than an hour's drive from the Louisiana Gulf Coast, where my dad found work in the oil industry after graduating from Tulane. Dad was a standout football player at Texas High School in Texarkana, Texas, and he received scholarship offers from the University of Texas and Texas A&M, among others. But on a visit to Tulane, he fell in love with the food of New Orleans and chose to play for the Green Wave.

Dad was a big guy—six foot three and 250 pounds as a defensive tackle in the mid-1970s—and he earned the nickname "Mean Gene" for how ferocious he was on opposing ball carriers. His Tulane teams had what they called a Big Hit Stick. Whenever the coaches noticed a tackle or a block on the game film that they deemed worthy of recognition, they awarded the player who had delivered the blow an opportunity to write his name on the Big Hit Stick. One season, despite missing most of the season with an injury, my dad signed his name to the stick more times than anyone else. I said he picked up his nickname because of how much he loved to hit people, but it wasn't always a player from the other team. Once, leading up to a game against Boston College, my dad got tired of hearing members of the media talk about how big and physical their opponent's offensive line was. During pregame warm-ups, he was so amped up to play that he hit one of his team's running backs and knocked him to the ground. Dad wrote his name on the Big Hit Stick after that game, but *not* for the hit on his teammate.

If not for repeated injuries, Dad could have played professionally. During his senior season, he was projected as a middle-round NFL draft pick before another knee injury ended his career.

As a youngster, when we visited my paternal grandparents in Texarkana, I was fascinated by an award my dad had won during his senior season at Tulane. To this day, I can close my eyes and visualize walking into my grandparents' home. From the front door to the right were two bedrooms and a bathroom. To the left was the kitchen, the dining area, an addition my grandfather built himself, and the main room. Against one wall in the main room, a large green-and-gold trophy with a TU logo sat on a mantel. I remember asking my dad what the trophy stood for, and he told me, "That's my captain's trophy that I got from Tulane."

I would stand beneath the mantel and stare up at that trophy. It looked humongous, and I remember thinking, *I want to be a big guy, I want to be strong, and I want to earn a trophy like Dad did.*

After Tulane, Dad started working at the Port of Lake Charles, unloading cargo from ships laden with shipping containers filled with pallets of rice, corn, and flour. He and his coworkers worked in pairs, lifting and throwing 110-pound sacks from those pallets for hours each day. Dad would come home covered in flour and tell Bryan and me about outworking his crew members throwing those heavy bags. Hearing him talk about how hard he worked only expanded my desire to be as strong as he was and to work as hard as he worked.

In his early days at the port, Dad worked with a couple of brothers, and they would invite him over to their house to eat. Their mother could cook up some tasty meals, and for a guy who chose his college based on food, his coworkers' home soon became a popular hangout spot. On one such visit, my dad was sitting on the couch when the guys' sister walked in and immediately captured his attention.

When she left the room, my dad asked the brothers, "Who's that?!"

"That's our sister Gilda." She was living in California with another sister and had come home to visit.

"Y'all didn't tell me you had another sister!" Dad said.

Before leaving that night, my dad tried to get Gilda's phone number, but she didn't seem interested and suggested that he get the number from her sister.

My dad got the number, and later, on a visit to Texarkana, he decided to give Gilda a call.

When my mom picked up the phone, my dad said, "Hey, this is Gene."

"Who?"

Dad's heart sank.

"You know, Gene. I met you at your parents' house."

Mom's response was along the lines of, "Oh, okay, whatever," so my dad had some work to do to gain her favor. Thankfully, he succeeded.

When my mom tells the story, she says the first thing she noticed was that my dad had one of his size 14 feet sticking straight up with the heel on the ground and the other foot resting on top of it. So her first impression was, *Who's the guy with the giant feet?*

I still get a kick out of hearing my parents tell their versions of their how-we-met story.

Thanks for persevering, Dad!

A Family That Played Together

In addition to working at the port, Dad also worked offshore on a platform for Shell Oil, spending a week or two at a time doing everything from working in the kitchen to driving a forklift to working on the crew boat.

Shortly before I turned six, Dad received a promotion to Shell's offices in One Shell Square (now the Hancock Whitney Center), a fifty-one-story skyscraper in New Orleans and the tallest building in Louisiana. Dad's new job was working in logistics and safety for the offshore platform. With the job change, our family moved to Slidell, northeast of New Orleans across Lake Pontchartrain. Dad woke up at 4:30 every morning to make the commute into the city.

Dad's "Mean Gene" nickname did not fit him outside of football. He is a humble, non-flashy guy who doesn't care about materialistic things. He is loyal and focused, and when he commits to something, he goes full force to get it done, even when it means extending himself beyond his comfort zone. Because of his focus, he can come across as intense when needed.

When Dad noticed Bryan or me getting off track on something like schoolwork, he leveraged that intensity to make sure we understood the importance and urgency of getting back on track. But he was intense like that because he was looking down the road for us, knowing that what he was pushing us to do would one day benefit us. He didn't need a lot of words to communicate because the words he chose were full of impact.

Mom is more laid-back than my dad. She has a gentle, quiet spirit. Dad handled most of the discipline at home, but Mom had a motherly way of letting us know we weren't doing right. More than telling us what we shouldn't do, she preferred to guide us to a better way of doing things. The exception to that gentle, quiet spirit came when Bryan and I didn't get our schoolwork done or got into fights. In those instances, she firmly took care of business.

The fights with Bryan, who is two years older than I am, were not anything more than the typical brother fights, but she hated them. "He's your only brother!" she would say. "You don't have anybody else, and y'all are arguing and fighting over this little thing."

Among Mom's go-to punishments was making us kneel in the corner and press our noses against the wall. That and hugs. Long hugs. She made us hug for extended lengths of time. During a forced hug, I would think, *This is my brother! I ain't going to hug this dude!* But, same as our dad, when Mom meant business, she didn't have to say much to get her point across.

Mom, who was also a very good athlete growing up, balanced our dad when it came to parenting us in sports. Especially because Bryan and I played the same sports my dad had played, he could really coach us up, whether in the yard or when he was coaching our teams. I think Mom advised Dad to tell us something only once that we needed to do on the field and then give us the opportunity to put his instructions into practice. As a result, even in my youth I developed into an athlete who would allow himself to make a mistake—*once*—as long as I learned from it. Then I kept those lessons learned in the forefront of my mind because I considered it careless to repeat a mistake.

Mom had eleven siblings. Dad was the youngest of three—and the only boy—in his family. Bryan is my only sibling, and I assumed my parents chose to have only two kids for financial reasons. Dad wanted to support our family in a way that enabled our mom not to work outside the home, so she could spend time with Bryan and me. Working offshore and at the port didn't net Dad a lot of money as the sole breadwinner, but it was enough to provide for us. Growing up, we never lacked for any cleats, uniforms, or equipment in the sports we played. He bought us used equipment—even my first bicycle came from a pawn shop—but we had what we needed.

Mom had her hands full staying home with two rambunctious boys, but she was up to the task. She had played basketball and softball in school, and while Dad was at work, she loved taking Bryan and me outside to play whatever sport was in season. During baseball season, she put on a glove and played catch with us. We didn't need to take anything off our fastballs when we were pitching to Mom. In basketball, she could shoot well and play defense against us out in the driveway. When it was football season, she threw passes to us. She also knew what a Cover 2 defense was and could spot an uncalled holding penalty from the stands. Because of her sports knowledge, she turned our outdoor games into coaching sessions.

"Let's work on fielding ground balls today," she might say to us. "At your last game, your dad was saying that sometimes you try to field the ball off to the side instead of getting in front of it."

We didn't just have fun practicing sports with our mom; we also improved as athletes from all those hours outside with her.

For most boys, their first momentous sports achievement comes when they beat their father in a sport for the first time. But for Bryan and me, our first milestone was defeating our mom. Only then could we advance to the next level of trying to beat Dad. One common thread with us Fortés is that we don't let our kids win just to let them win. I learned that from my parents, and I'm the same way with my own kids. And they are not going to beat me for a long time!

I'm sure my mom had dreams and aspirations that she sacrificed to stay home with Bryan and me. In fact, after we were both out of the house—and out of her hair—she took a job selling jewelry at JCPenney. Although she didn't have a formal job while I was growing up, I saw her work ethic around the house. She kept our home clean, and she always cooked for us. She also drove us to practices and games and never complained about building her calendar around our schedules.

Pouring the Foundation

Dad found ways to teach Bryan and me lessons even through seemingly mundane tasks.

Our home sat among some tall pine trees. Pine trees are evergreens, so they don't drop leaves in the fall; but all that means is they are constantly shedding old pine needles to make room for new ones. Some people like the look of brown pine needles spread across their yards. But my dad would always clear away the needles. I don't know if he didn't like the look or was just trying to stay busy, but he would often rake the fallen needles into piles in our front and side yards. Occasionally he would tell Bryan and me that he needed to go somewhere for a couple of hours, and he wanted all the piles picked up by the time he got home. My brother and I removed needles from our yard so often that we developed a sweet system to save time. At first, one of us would hold a trash bag open while the other scooped needles into the bag. But then we figured out that we could cut our time in half by each filling our own bag. So we split up, placing a bag between our heels and using our hands to scoop the pine needles into the bag. He and I might have complained a little while we worked, but we got the job done because Dad said he wanted a clean yard. Even as we grew older, cutting the grass and other chores were just part of living in the Forté house. In case you've never visited southern Louisiana, the summers are long, hot, and humid; so we not only learned what it meant to work hard but also how to work hard in difficult conditions. Despite the heat and humidity, Bryan and I could be counted on to finish our work because we saw the sacrifices our parents made for us. Dad spent almost every day with us doing some type of sport after he returned home from work, whether coaching our teams, throwing us passes in the yard, shooting hoops in the driveway, or sitting on a bucket in the strip of land between our house and our neighbor's house to catch while we practiced pitching for baseball season. He often waited to have dinner until after a practice ended. So we wanted to do what we could to make things easier for him, considering how hard he worked during the week and how much time he devoted to our sports.

Dad often told us that effort doesn't require talent. After Bryan and I started playing organized sports, we learned—and heard over and over again—the coach's cliché that hard work beats talent when talent doesn't work hard. Dad lived by that motto. He possessed a set of gifts and skills, but he also worked hard to allow his two sons to excel.

More than anything else our parents did for us, they modeled the importance of faith. My mom grew up Catholic, and my dad's father pastored a Baptist church in the small town of Hooks, Texas, near Texarkana. Bryan and I attended a Catholic Sunday school and the Sunday service at a Methodist church, up until the time of our Catholic confirmation and First Communion. After that, we attended only the Methodist church.

Looking back, I consider my younger years of faith a season of life when my roots were shallow. Religion was more of a routine for me, and faith was an add-on to my life rather than the core. But from the Catholic emphasis on routines, the importance of consistently attending church carried me through high school and into college, where the roots of my faith began to grow deeper. I needed time to learn that being a Christian was not about checking off boxes for tasks completed, that Christianity was all about having a relationship with God. But I'm grateful for the faith foundation that was laid for me in growing up a Forté.

2

SENSE OF PURPOSE

From as far back as I can recall, football has intrigued me. My dad would tell his friends that I was the only three-year-old he'd ever seen who could sit quietly for three hours if a football game was on television. I don't remember watching other sports on TV when I was a kid. Just football.

Perhaps I was drawn to the physical nature of the game—the speed, the intensity. Whatever the reason, the sport was intertwined with the image of my dad, a giant of a man to my young eyes. Dad didn't sit around reminiscing about his glory days in football; but as I grew older, became more curious, and started asking questions, I learned more about him as a player and as a man. Watching and talking football with my dad and then seeing those big men on the TV screen made football something I wanted to play too.

I first saw football in person after we moved to Slidell when I was six. One day our family was riding bikes in John Slidell Park, and I saw some kids about my size, in full pads, practicing football. My dad walked over and learned about the Slidell Youth Football Association (SYFA). Kids as young as five could play, and the league played games on Saturdays on three fields. Texas, Louisiana's big neighbor, is known for its love of football at all levels. But my home state also takes the sport pretty seriously.

When Dad shared what he had learned about the youth league, I told him I wanted to play.

"You're a little bit young to start playing football," he said. "How about you wait a year?"

My response was out of line, and out of character, but it reflected my growing passion for the game.

"No!" I said emphatically. "I want to play football *now*. I see those boys playing. Why can't I do what they're doing? I'm their size, and *their* parents let them play."

"Who are you, talking to me like that?" my dad replied. "I'm your father. Don't be talking crazy to me."

That shut down further discussion but only increased my desire.

Knowing what I know now about my dad's career and the injuries and surgeries, I can understand his reluctance to sign me up at such a young age. He might have been trying to protect me. But at that moment, all I knew was that I wanted to play football, and he said I couldn't.

The following year, when I was seven, Dad took me to the football sign-ups. Though Bryan was nine, he was on the fence about playing, so he didn't sign up; and Dad was completely fine with that. I learned a lesson from my dad that I follow now as a father: I will not force my kids to play sports just because I was successful as an athlete. I will support and cheer for them in whatever endeavors they pursue as they grow up.

With a population of about 25,000 then, Slidell was large enough to have its own youth league, and the league was pretty hardcore. Players were placed in divisions based on their age and weight. The division for five- to seven-year-olds had a weight limit of seventy pounds, as I recall. Any kid over that threshold would be placed in a division with mostly older kids. Registration was held at the Kmart off one of the main streets in town. When Dad took me to sign up, we saw kids who must have been slightly over the weight limit running in the Kmart parking lot wearing trash bags. In theory, the plastic would cause them to sweat more and allow them to make weight for their preferred division. (Note to kids *and* parents: Do not do this! Wearing a trash bag while working out can cause dehydration!) I was average size for my age then, so making weight was not a concern for me.

After the sign-up, the next step was like a mini–NFL Combine. The players ran through some drills, and the coaches made selections based on who they wanted to draft onto their teams. The tryouts provided the coaches an opportunity to scout the players and develop a draft strategy. Each kid sprinted about twenty yards, then lined up and ran a route to catch a pass. Then that same kid threw the ball to a coach. Essentially, those were three quick drills for evaluating the boys' athleticism and skills. If a kid displayed good speed and decent throwing form, he became a candidate to play quarterback. If a kid had good size but dropped his pass or wasn't fast, he would become an offensive or defensive lineman. If a kid showed some speed and good hands in catching his pass but threw the ball awkwardly back to the coach, he would be a running back or receiver on offense or a defensive back or linebacker on defense. After the evaluation session, the coaches gathered to hold their draft.

A coach named Terry Firman drafted me to play for the Tigers, and my dad volunteered as an assistant coach. While on the team, I met Coach Firman's son Scott, who continued playing football with me throughout high school and remains a good friend to this day.

In his two-back offense, Coach Firman made me one of the running backs. The other back, Jarell Adams, had played football before and was one of the kids on the cusp of being too big for our division. He was also the kid who knocked me flat on my back on my first carry in practice. With Jarell's size and my speed, we had a thunder-and-lighting combination in our backfield.

As a retired NFL player, I can look back on my youth playing days and appreciate the opportunity to play both offense and defense. That primarily ended in high school because I was deemed too important to our offense to risk injury on defense.

Playing in the SYFA was fun because there wasn't much to figure out on the field. On defense, for example, all we had to do was hit and tackle. I played cornerback before moving to safety, where I intercepted a few passes even though a passing game was pretty rare at that age level. Eventually I was shifted to linebacker, where I could be involved in more plays.

Our division had a rule banning defenses from blitzing. My dad called the defensive plays, and he found a loophole in the rules that he exploited when I played safety. He occasionally called a play in which I moved up from my normal position to about five yards from the line of scrimmage. Then I would anticipate the snap so I could sprint through the line and into the backfield to tackle the ball carrier for a loss. But Dad had to limit the number of times he called that play so they wouldn't change the rule.

I loved playing defense. My dad and brother both played defense, and throughout my career, I often wondered what it would be like to play safety with my size. (Most players in the NFL believe they could play just as well on the opposite side of the ball. Whether they're correct or not is a different matter!) My own speculation didn't venture too far past the thought of a running back my size breaking through the second level of the defense. As the safety, I would have to guess whether the ball carrier would try to juke me or run me over like a truck. Truth be told, I preferred to be the one with the ball making the juke-or-truck decision. Plus, I knew running back was my best position.

Studying the Best

Although my family lived about thirty miles from the Superdome, I was never a Saints fan because in those years they weren't winning many games. I didn't have a favorite team, but I had a favorite position that I followed. I was a fan of running backs.

I recorded the *NFL Yearbook* shows on TV—thirty-minute episodes that presented an NFL team's highlights from the previous season. It was all set to music and built around a theme. I recorded the yearbook for every team in the league. For most teams, the highlights heavily featured the running back. That was the NFL's "bell cow" era for running backs, when teams relied heavily on their top back to handle a large workload during games. Offenses were built around running the ball, and it wasn't uncommon for a lead back to get twenty, sometimes thirty, carries in a game, plus a screen pass or two.

Among the running backs I studied the most were Marshall Faulk, who was from New Orleans and played for the Indianapolis Colts and St. Louis Rams; Emmitt Smith of the Dallas Cowboys, partly because my dad was a Texas guy; Marcus Allen of the Los Angeles Raiders and Kansas City Chiefs, who was adept at both rushing and receiving; and Barry Sanders of the Detroit Lions, another do-it-all back. I studied how they carried the ball, their mannerisms, and especially their moves. Whenever one of them talked about the running back position, I listened for anything I could learn from the best-of-the-best playing the position I envisioned playing someday in their league.

I remember watching one running back who was big for his position and also fast. Because of his size, he had the ability to run over defensive players; but sometimes he made a move to get around a tackler who appeared to be expecting a collision. By my second or third year of youth football, I was not necessarily taller than most of the kids, but my frame was thicker. I could run with a physical style or take advantage of my speed and agility. From watching that other running back, I decided to start my games by running over a defender or two to establish that physical expectation for the defense and then switch to setting up tacklers for a move that would lead to a longer run or, hopefully, a touchdown.

I also remember one of those shows that featured wide receiver Terrell Owens while he was playing for the 49ers. The cameras showed T. O. at home working out late at night. I remember he was doing a bunch of sit-ups. I wondered why he was working out so late. Then he told the camera operator to look at the clock on the wall. It was almost midnight.

"See," he said, "everybody's sleeping, but I'm here working." Then the next morning, he was up early and reporting to the team facility before any of his teammates.

Seeing T. O.'s work ethic inspired me. I was determined to outwork every other kid across the country who wanted to become a great running back. I also realized there were kids who wanted to become great defensive players—and who knew when I might meet up with one of them in a game? My success in that moment just might come down to the one day he decided to slack off and I didn't.

Learning to Look Ahead

My dad coached me every year until high school, and he was my head coach beginning with the second or third year I played.

I loved playing for my dad, not only because of who he was but also because he was a very good coach. His team was known as the one you wanted to play for, or the team to beat, and we won a few championships along the way.

One of my favorite coach-son moments came when I was eleven or twelve. Though most of the players in the league by then had been playing for five or six years, passing was still a risky proposition. To be successful, every offensive lineman had to make his block, the quarterback had to deliver an accurate pass, and the receiver had to catch it. That's asking a lot from a group of eleven- and twelve-year-olds. Like most teams in our league, we relied primarily on our running game.

Dad, however, was looking ahead to an upcoming game against a rival team that could determine the league champion. He installed a special package in case we were trailing in the game and needed to move the ball downfield in a hurry. He made wristbands with the new plays on them so we could quickly call plays while the clock was running. In the new package, he moved me to quarterback because I had a good, accurate arm from being a pitcher in baseball. But I would be quarterback in a shotgun formation, which added another element of risk for our age—the shotgun snap.

When we practiced the special plays, something went wrong more often than not. A receiver would run the wrong route. The snap from the center would be off, causing a fumble or throwing off the timing of the play. Robert, one of the other running backs on our team, had talent but seemed to have trouble catching the easy balls. When he was well covered or a defender got a hand up in front of him, Robert dependably made the catch. But if you removed those obstacles and the challenge they presented, he usually dropped the pass. There was no way my dad could draw up a play that intentionally created a difficult catch scenario.

Sure enough, in the game against our rival, we trailed by six points late in the fourth quarter. Facing third and long from our own 30 yard line, Dad put us in our special package, and I moved to quarter-back. The play called for Robert to line up as a receiver and run a deep out pattern so he could catch the ball for the first down and get out of bounds to stop the clock. I threw a beautiful pass that hit Robert squarely in the hands. You can guess the outcome.

That gave us a fourth-and-long situation, and at that stage in the game there was no question that we would go for the first down. We had no other option. The play called for the receivers on the right side to run out routes to take their defenders with them toward the sideline. Robert lined up to the left at receiver to run a post route—head straight down the field and then cut toward the goal post at a forty-five-degree angle. The pass had to go to Robert.

I took the snap, and while I was giving Robert time to get downfield and make his cut to the middle of the field, the blocking on the offensive line broke down. I spun and started to run. When the rushing defenders reacted to that move, I stepped up into the pocket. The out routes had drawn most of the secondary toward the right sideline, according to plan, and only one defender remained with Robert. I saw him make his cut to the post, and for some reason the lone defender seemed uncertain about whether he was supposed to stay with Robert. Robert was now wide open, breaking to the middle of the field. I threw the ball about as far as I could. My pass looked on target, and it would be an easy catch for any receiver to make. Which, of course, made it a difficult catch for Robert. I watched as my pass dropped right into Robert's hands . . . and he secured the ball and took off running for the end zone. We made the extra point to defeat our rival with an exciting, improbable, one-point victory.

When Dad had started installing the new plays in our practices, I didn't think we would ever be trailing late in a game and need to run them. Also, based on the outcome of those plays in practice, I wasn't confident they would work even if we needed them. I thought we'd be better off relying on our usual running game to win.

Walking off the field toward the sideline, I saw my dad looking at me. His facial expression and body language were saying, "Yes, Son, I do know a little bit about football. So trust my coaching."

I remember that game and that play so vividly not only because we won the game in exciting fashion but because my dad had looked farther ahead in the season than we players were looking. And he implemented a package of plays that allowed us to win, even if I—and who knows who else on the team—felt we could not complete such a pass. Dad saw in us an ability we didn't know we had.

Football history is filled with miraculous plays to win games. The original "Hail Mary" pass by Doug Flutie at Boston College. "The Catch" from Joe Montana to Dwight Clark for the San Francisco 49ers against Dallas. The Tennessee Titans' "Music City Miracle." But for my money, Robert's catch on the post route ranks right up there at the top.

Discovering the Gift

I've described how my collision with Jarell in my first practice, and my reaction to it, became a defining moment in my life. Another moment that proved pivotal also occurred during my first season of youth football, in a conversation with my dad.

After our second or third game, and with a few touchdowns under my belt, I asked my dad a question that surprised him: "When I get the football and I'm running and they come to tackle me, can I move out of the way?"

"What are you talking about?" he replied. "Yeah, you can avoid the tackler. I thought you knew that."

When Dad tells that story, he says that once I learned that it was okay to make moves to avoid getting hit by defenders, my game soared to a new level. He still has film from those days that illustrate the difference. When I made it to the NFL, guys I played with back home and stayed in contact with told me that they would watch me on TV and recognize some of my moves as the same ones I made in SYFA games.

I'm not exaggerating when I say that I could tell at age seven that

I had been given a gift, and it started after I learned that I could try to elude defenders.

Running with a football came naturally to me—it's the only thing in my life for which I could say without hesitation, "I know how to do this." I had a running back's sense of the field. I could see a defender coming toward me and instinctively know how to set him up for a move that would make him miss me. I sensed oncoming tacklers before I could see them in my peripheral vision. I felt as if I could not be tackled. (I said *felt*. I was tackled plenty of times.)

My dad saved game film from those days, and I was executing spin moves and jump cuts that no one had ever taught me. Moves I later made as a professional, I was already making at age seven. They obviously came at a different speed and level of play when I was a kid, but looking at those game films, I can see the earliest version of what I would become as a running back.

I was not surprised by what I could do running the ball on a football field. That wasn't a pride issue for me. I could not explain how I knew what to do. But because of my faith background, I recognized that the Lord had blessed me with a talent in football and the ability to use it. From then on, the focus of my life became trying to figure out the reason for the gift.

Did God design me to play running back? For what purpose?

3

FOLLOWING MY PASSION

There's a difference between love and passion. Growing up, I loved playing a variety of sports—baseball, basketball, and soccer—in addition to football. During high school, I made decisions to leave behind other sports I loved in order to pursue my true passion.

Football.

My freshman year at Slidell High, I played football, basketball, and baseball. I probably could have played beyond high school in baseball as a pitcher and a hitter if I had stayed with the sport, but I quit baseball after my freshman year because the season overlapped with spring football practice. I played basketball for two years in high school before making football my sole focus.

I picked up track as a sophomore, but only to help me in football. When I talked to the track coach about joining the team, I told him I didn't want to run in meets; I only wanted to use the workouts to get faster. He said okay. But then in practice, when I participated in mock relays to help our team prepare for meets, I started outrunning the varsity runner on my leg of the relay. Afterward, the coach told me, "You've got to run in meets." So I did. Then I started winning 100-meter and 200-meter races. I consistently ran 10.3 or 10.4 in the 100. I could have lowered my times by dropping a bit of weight, because I was heavier than the best sprinters. But my purpose for running track was to become faster as a football player, and I stayed true to that purpose and never considered shedding any weight to see how much I could lower my times.

My freshman year of football, I played on the freshman and junior varsity teams and dressed out for a few varsity games without getting into a game. My brother was a junior on the varsity and one of the team's best defensive players.

Occasionally, non-varsity players were called over to the varsity practice to run scout team against the starters, simulating that week's opponents' offensive and defensive formations and plays. The preparation was more mental than physical, intended to give the varsity players a preview of what they would see during the game. As such, the varsity guys were more focused on making sure they lined up correctly and knew their assignments than making plays or getting physical.

For a young player like me with varsity aspirations, running scout team allowed me to show the varsity coaches my capabilities against their best players. So, going up against varsity defenders not too interested in tackling a freshman running back, I treated scout team like a varsity tryout, making moves and not backing down from contact even though there was a noticeable size difference between me and the seniors and juniors. Bryan, as one of the team's leaders, would razz his teammates when I showed them up.

"My brother is doing this to y'all?" he'd ask loud enough for anyone on the practice field to hear. I knew what the varsity guys were—and were not—trying to get from practicing against the scout team, but it was still cool to know that my brother saw what I could do and to feel that public validation from him.

My sophomore year, I started at running back on the JV team, killed it on Thursday nights against that level of competition, and also dressed out for all the Friday night varsity games. On varsity, the coaches played me at fullback, on special teams, and a little at linebacker. That year, our school switched from the Wing-T offense it had run for years to a mostly Pro-Style offense with a bit of Spread mixed in. The funny thing is, my dad had been hoping the coaches would change our offense by the time I made varsity, because a Wing-T offense in college was rare and, thus, was not good preparation for playing running back at the next level.

The Wing-T is an old-school offense with three running backs and very little passing. In fact, if a team has the Wing-T clicking and grinding out yardage, it can go an entire game without attempting a pass. A typical Pro-Style offense, by contrast, has two running backs, with one the featured back, or main ball carrier, and the other a full-back, whose main responsibility is to block. A Pro-Style offense tends to provide more balance between the running and passing games. A Spread offense usually has one running back in the backfield and can lean more pass heavy. But with the right personnel, the Spread can still be a highly effective offense for featuring the run game.

Playing fullback was humbling because I had to block for our main running back, who was a senior, instead of carrying the ball myself. Occasionally, I had my number called on a screen play, so I touched the ball every now and then.

One of my special teams roles was the personal protector on the punt team. I was the guy who lined up in the backfield, about five yards behind the line, and prevented any defensive player who broke through from getting to our punter and blocking his kick. Although I didn't want to play fullback, that year of blocking for our running back and punter gave me an appreciation for the players whose full-time job is blocking for others and those who sacrifice their aspirations to make careers out of being good on special teams.

I adopted an attitude of doing whatever job the coaches wanted me to do to help our team. I could have gone to my dad and said about the other running back, “I’m better than that guy, but I’ve got to block for him.” Or “Man, they’ve got me spending my time on special teams.” I never did that, but I admit it was not always easy. That season, I learned about patience and how to be a good teammate even if you’re not the guy getting all the carries, yards, touchdowns, and attention.

The little bit I played on defense wound up helping me as a running back as well, because we ran physical drills in practice that focused on hitting and shedding blocks. Those drills made me unafraid of contact.

My Brother’s Inspiration

Without a doubt, the highlight of my sophomore year was sharing the field with my brother for his senior season. I had been on the sideline with him in the varsity games I dressed for the year before, but it was a totally different experience practicing with him every day and being between the lines with him under the Friday night lights. I enjoyed watching Bryan lead on the field. He was a quiet leader but became more vocal when needed.

In high school football, two years of age makes a significant difference in size, speed, agility, and power. I was the tailback when we ran scout team for goal-line situations, and every once in a while Bryan would get a shot at trying to prevent me from scoring.

Boom.

As Dad said, that’s football. Plus, it made me a better player for when I would be the varsity running back going up against the other team’s “Bryan.”

My brother and I were always competitive with each other growing up, but it was a healthy type of competition with no pride or jealousy involved.

When I signed up for football at age seven, Bryan wasn't sure he wanted to play, and so he didn't. But after seeing how much fun I was having, Bryan decided to play the following year. Because of how much I looked up to Bryan as my big brother and how I strived to be like him in sports, I found satisfaction in learning that I had inspired him to take up football.

Bryan possessed more natural talent than I did, but we were both good athletes who loved to win. We also both wanted to be the best player on the field. It was no different when we competed head-to-head, but we always rooted for each other.

In youth baseball, for example, when we were in different leagues because of our ages, our parents had us sit with them in the stands to support each other, instead of letting us run off to hang out with our friends. I remember watching Bryan play baseball, which wasn't his best sport. You could see his natural athletic ability on the field, but he had yet to develop some of the baseball-specific skills. He was an outfielder at an age when not many batted balls made it to the outfield on the fly. Bryan was a little awkward in the beginning, and Dad worked tirelessly with him at home to teach him, first, not to be afraid of a ball hit high in the air, and then how to catch pop-ups.

I think Bryan was in center field for one particular game, and a fly ball was hit to him. He positioned himself to make the catch and stuck his glove up in the air as the ball came down toward him. If you've ever seen Scotty Smalls's first catch in the movie *The Sandlot*, you've basically seen Bryan's catch as well. Dad jumped about five feet off the ground and let out a big "Yeah!"

Bryan's main sport was football, and his strength was clearly evident on defense, where he gained a reputation as a big hitter.

He instinctively knew how to read and diagnose plays, and then he would just fly to the ball.

In a junior high game against Lee Road, when Bryan was on the kickoff team, he hit their kick returner so hard that I would not be surprised if that kid retired from football that night. When we got the film from that game, we looked up that play just to see if we had actually seen what we thought we had. One of the enduring images from that film was of a Lee Road coach on the sideline reacting to Bryan's hit by grabbing the top of his head with both hands, as if he were saying, "Oh my gosh!"

I have always considered it an advantage to be the younger brother. Bryan made it that way because he never tired of me following him around and playing pickup games and riding bikes with his friends. Or at least he never told me. Being two years younger, I felt that if I could keep up with Bryan and his friends, I would be competing at a higher level compared to the rest of the kids my age.

Playing against Bryan and his friends toughened me up because of the size difference between us. And they didn't take it easy on me. Because Bryan was bigger and stronger, he roughed me up more than a few times. His friends thought they could rough me up as well, but I wasn't taking anything from them. If a pickup game got physical, I wouldn't start anything; but if someone else chose to mix it up, I had no problem finishing matters. I remember one day when Bryan walked into our house complaining, "Mom, Matthew's beating up my friends."

As my big brother, Bryan set a standard of talent and hard work for me to follow. I paid particular attention to his work ethic in the school's weight room. My freshman year, he was in the varsity group lifting weights, and I made a mental note of how much he was bench-pressing—275 pounds as a junior. When I benched 285 my junior year, I felt a big-time sense of accomplishment. In a way, I beat him in the weight room, and that's an example of the healthy competition between us. If Bryan had been there that day, I know he would have felt a touch of sadness that I had beaten his weight, but I also know he would have been pumped up and high-fiving me.

I'm grateful that Bryan chose to be the type of big brother who allowed me to compete with him in a healthy way and to learn lessons from him.

Bryan earned a starting linebacker spot on the varsity team as a freshman. During his junior year, he started receiving attention from college coaches, though Slidell High had never been a hotbed for college recruiting. Our two claims to fame were Reggie Cooper, who won All-America honors in three sports in the mid-1980s, played football and baseball at Nebraska, and appeared in two games with the Dallas Cowboys; and Brett Bech, who walked on at LSU, led the Tigers in receptions for two seasons, and played three years in the NFL with the Saints. Our program wasn't known for making deep playoff runs, so college recruiters weren't hanging out on campus to check out our players.

The recruiting letters that came for Bryan bore the logos of big-name programs like LSU, Nebraska, Auburn, and Colorado. He read every one, and I read them after him, envisioning those letters coming addressed to me. Despite Bryan's talent, he was considered too short to receive a scholarship offer from the major programs. He was a shade under six feet tall and weighed 220 pounds.

Recruiters have size requirements they look for, and at the NCAA Division I-A level they wanted linebackers to be at least six feet tall. I never understood why so many sports decisions were based solely on a player's size. Bryan was not quite the height they wanted—by half an inch!—but he powerlifted, played basketball, and competed in track and field as a sprinter and shot-putter. He was fast and strong, but he didn't quite meet their height requirement.

Bryan wound up playing for McNeese State, in Lake Charles, Louisiana. But in a scrimmage before the start of his freshman year, he broke his leg and dislocated his ankle playing on a muddy field. Though he recovered from that injury, he was never quite the same player again. When he suffered a knee injury during his junior year, I could see how the injury—and the rehab required to come back from it—took a toll on him. He opted not to play his senior year but stayed in school to complete his degree. He never acted sad about how his career ended, and he remained one of my three biggest supporters.

For Mom and Dad

My junior season, I shared the backfield with a senior in a two–running back system, but the coaches made me the primary ball carrier. After waiting to start at running back and adding in a year of experience for our team in the new offense, I was ready to take over games.

My dad was ready for me to take over, too, apparently. He liked to sit at the base of the press box because that was the closest to a coach's view he could get from the stands. Coach Artie Liuzza, our offensive coordinator, who had played with my dad at Tulane, called plays from the coaches' booth in the press box, directly above where my dad sat.

Dad was known for making statements loud enough for the coaches in the box to hear. Things like, "It's third and three. This is a good time for a screen." Or if we were near the goal line, "You've got a two-hundred-pound running back. Run the ball." Dad told me about times when he would suggest a call and then we ran that play. I don't know whether his former teammate could hear him or not. Coach Liuzza became the head coach at Slidell a few years after I graduated, and in 2009 he was inducted into the St. Bernard Parish Sports Hall of Fame—all without my dad's help—so perhaps it was just a case of two good coaching minds thinking alike.

Our team won the district championship and finished the regular season with a 10–0 record, ranked number seven in the state in

Class 5A (Louisiana's largest classification). We earned the number two seed for the state playoffs. In the first round, we played a home game against Fontainebleau High School from nearby Mandeville. We fell behind 17–7 after Fontainebleau scored touchdowns on a punt return and an interception. There was no way our undefeated team should lose a first-round game on our home field. Fortunately, we took control of the game to win 49–17.

In the regional round, we squared off against Carencro, a team that had spent part of the season ranked above us in the state poll before finishing at number nine. We defeated them rather handily, 33–13. Though I didn't have a big night statistically, I crossed the 1,000-yard rushing mark for the season. More important for my football future, this was the night two coaches from Tulane saw me play for the first time. Not until my senior year would my dad begin sending out game film, so I don't think any colleges were aware of me at this point. Tulane's coaches were there to watch one of my teammates on defense. The timing could not have been any better for my recruiting prospects because of what happened in the next round of the playoffs.

In the quarterfinals, we had to bus almost 300 miles upstate to play West Monroe at their home stadium in northern Louisiana. Though we were undefeated and West Monroe was 9–3, I doubt most followers of Louisiana high school football expected us to win against a team that had finished the previous season as state runner-up and had won five state titles over the past decade. Indeed, the Rebels proved to be too much for us that night. We trailed 27–0 in the second quarter and ended our season with a 41–15 loss. West Monroe went on to finish second in the state, losing 21–20 to Evangel in the final.

My season ended a couple hours earlier than my teammates'. On my first carry of the game, I was tackled after a two-yard gain. When I went down, my ankle got caught under someone else in the pile.

I hopped to the sideline on my good leg, and our trainers examined me. They determined that there wasn't a fracture, but my ankle was severely sprained. The trainers iced my ankle to try to stop the swelling and numb the pain. Then they wrapped the ankle in tape for extra support. I wanted to go back into the game so badly, and I tried to jog on the sideline to test my ankle, but it was clearly a no-go.

After a loss of that magnitude, the bus ride home seemed much longer than the ride up had been. We had turned in one of Slidell's best seasons in a long time and came within two wins of playing in the state championship game. Personally, I had displayed my ability to both run and catch the ball, after rushing for 1,057 yards with eight touchdowns and catching thirty passes for 365 yards and three touchdowns. As a result, I began to attract my first interest from college recruiters.

To me, recruiting was about more than just football. I saw earning a football scholarship as a way to honor my parents for the sacrifices they had made for Bryan and me. I hadn't forgotten the day, heading into Bryan's senior year, when I had seen my dad working on our home computer.

"What are you doing?" I asked.

"See this?" Dad said, pointing to a dollar amount on the screen.

"Yes."

"This is your and your brother's college fund."

"That's it?"

"Yeah," he said. "You see there's not a lot of money in there, so y'all better work hard and pray that you get a scholarship."

4

ALL IT TAKES IS ONE

Rivals was the dominant source of college recruiting news when I was in high school, and they rated me a two-star recruit on their five-star scale. That means they considered me a player suited for a mid-major conference team. Using today's college football terminology, it would be a school in one of the Group of Five conferences: the American Athletic Conference, Conference USA, Mid-American Conference, Mountain West Conference, or Sun Belt Conference.

I didn't have a preferred college I wanted to attend, but I knew I wanted to play at a big school—whether close to home at LSU (which is about ninety miles from Slidell) or someplace far away, like USC, Ohio State, or Florida. Those were the teams playing on TV on Saturdays, and I viewed schools like those as a launching pad to the NFL.

Before my senior season of high school, I attended camps at Auburn and LSU.

Auburn was about a five-hour drive from Slidell, and a friend from another high school invited me to ride with him to the camp. It was held during Auburn's spring practices, so I was able to see their three elite running backs—Ronnie Brown, Brandon Jacobs, and Cadillac Williams—in action. All three would make it to the NFL, and between them, they accounted for almost 15,000 rushing yards in the league. As a high school kid, I was fascinated by how they warmed up and practiced—all on the same field for the same team. Envisioning myself in their spot a little more than a year later did not feel like a stretch to me.

During the summer, I attended LSU's camp—*the* camp for Louisiana high school players—which was run by Nick Saban, who was the head coach then. I remember how, at the start of camp, all these guys, some of whom were elite athletes, were thinking the camp would be easy—I guess because we wouldn't be wearing pads, we'd just be learning football. Or so they assumed. Far from it! The camp was two or three days long, and we *worked.* The morning after the first day, guys were moving gingerly around the campus dorm where we were staying, complaining about how sore they were.

It wasn't unusual during camp for one of the campers to report to the rest of us that he had just been offered a scholarship by one of the LSU coaches. That was everyone's dream. I had a great camp, and the running backs coach, Derek Dooley, told me I was "really good" but that they didn't have an opening on their roster for a running back from my class.

Both camps were filled with four- and five-star recruits—the most highly touted college prospects—but other than the number of stars in their ratings and the attention they received, I honestly could not see a difference between them and me. When I saw one of the guys drop a pass or not run full speed in a drill, I wondered, *What makes him a five-star?*

I came to realize how much recruiting resembles marketing.

Who was ranking all these players anyway? There was no way every high school player assigned a star had received a proper evaluation. Instead, the four- and five-star awards tended to be affixed to players from the bigger or more notable high school programs, or to those whose names appeared in the newspaper sports section the most. I learned not to put much stock in the ranking systems and the outside opinions that created and maintained them. I knew what type of player I was, and all I needed was for one school to give me a chance.

My senior year, our team was unable to follow up on the previous year's success of an undefeated regular season. We won the district championship, finished the regular season with an 8–2 record, and carried a six-game winning streak into the postseason. But we were seeded sixteenth overall and were eliminated in the first round with a 28–16 loss to Destrehan.

I was the focal point of our offense and had a great season individually, rushing for 1,375 yards and twenty-three touchdowns. I rushed for more than 200 yards in a couple of games and scored five touchdowns in a game. I also caught eighteen passes for 253 yards and two TDs. I was selected as our district's Offensive Most Valuable Player, the St. Tammany Parish Player of the Year, and second team all-state.

With that success came individual attention, like having my name in the paper and some of my touchdown runs shown on the local TV stations on Friday nights.

After home games, I would shower, get dressed, and step outside to head home, only to see young kids waiting for me so they could ask for my autograph. I didn't understand why they would want an ink scribble from me, but I happily honored every request because of a childhood experience of my own.

I am a distant cousin of Sam Adams, who played fourteen seasons in the NFL as a defensive lineman. When I was eleven, Sam was with the Seattle Seahawks, and they played a game against the Saints in the Superdome. I went with members of my family—it was the only NFL game I attended until my rookie year with the Bears. Sam got us access to the area where the team buses parked, and after the game we were waiting there to talk to him. I noticed some other kids asking players for autographs as they walked past to their buses, so I walked over to join them. I had never asked for anyone's autograph before, but it seemed like it might be something cool.

As one Saints player walked toward us on his way to the buses, I asked, "Can I get your autograph?"

"I don't have time, kid," he said as he kept walking.

He was the only player I saw say no to any of us kids. I remember thinking, *He ain't even that good of a player, and he won't give us an autograph?*

Because of that experience, I have never turned down a kid's request for an autograph. I don't want anyone to experience what I felt that day in the Superdome. Now, if it's an adult who I've noticed keeps coming back for more autographs, I *will* say no, because that's somebody trying to make money off the athletes' signatures.

In high school, as more people became familiar with my name, the place where I struggled the most with the attention I received was unexpected. It was my church. I think everyone at church on Sunday morning had read the Saturday paper and knew how our team had done on Friday night and my stats for the game. The pastor occasionally mentioned my accomplishments from the pulpit. Sometimes he even included me in his sermon. Whenever he mentioned my name, the people in the pews turned to look at me. For an introvert who doesn't like the spotlight, it made me so uncomfortable that I wanted to crawl under my pew.

I understood that everyone just wanted me to know they were proud of me. Slidell was a small community, and I was one of their kids. They knew my family and had watched Bryan and me grow up.

So I appreciated the love they showed me. But at the same time, I didn't see it as a good thing when the pastor mentioned my football accomplishments right before dismissing the service, and when my Friday night achievements were what everyone wanted to talk about on the way out of church.

Shouldn't they be remembering the verses that the pastor preached on? I remember thinking a few times, *I'm not Jesus!*

Still, I believe my faith kept me grounded amid the growing publicity. Our family was in church every Sunday, and throughout high school I attended Friday morning breakfasts hosted by our school's Fellowship of Christian Athletes (FCA). Honestly, the free breakfast of eggs, grits, sausage, and bacon—lots of bacon—was the main motivation for getting to school an hour early on Fridays. The FCA folks were smart enough to wait until after their talk to feed us!

As I look back on my high school days, I can see that my faith was surface level—more of an add-on to my life instead of being the center. It's as if I believed—or perhaps *hoped* is the better word—that if I went to the FCA breakfast on Friday morning, I would play a good game that night. But even though my faith hadn't yet grown deep roots, I still had the solid foundation instilled by my family. Yes, religion was more of a routine for me then, but I was in church every Sunday, I was at the FCA breakfasts, and I was hearing God's Word shared on a regular basis. The seed of my faith was growing beneath the surface.

Making the Easy Choice

I provided my dad with plenty of good game film to send out to college coaches, and a few wrote back expressing interest in me. But looking back, we started too late in the recruiting cycle to land a scholarship offer from one of the major programs. A coach from Virginia Tech wrote to me, "Thank you for sending us your game film." And then he added the "but" that I was getting used to hearing.

"You're an exceptional player, but we've already offered all our scholarships for running backs."

I also battled against being projected as a college fullback. I was six feet, two hundred pounds by my junior year, but I didn't have a fullback-type body; so I didn't understand why I kept being slotted there. In my view at the time, the fullback was basically a glorified offensive lineman, whose primary role was to block out of the backfield, and that's not what I wanted. Since my very first practice at age seven, I had recognized I had a special gift for running the ball. I was an elusive runner who was also good at catching the ball. Turning me into a fullback would not be the best use of what I could do on the field.

I was so resolute about being a running back that I wasn't interested in talking to any college that wanted to recruit me as a fullback—including one school in the elite Southeastern Conference.

Our varsity coach, Wayne Grubb, had told me that someone from Mississippi State had talked to him about me and would be coming to our high school campus to meet with me in person. I was in class one day when a person from the front office interrupted over the loudspeaker and asked me to come down. As I walked through the hallway, I began to get excited about meeting with the coach. Mississippi State was the type of school I wanted to play for.

When I walked into the office, Coach Grubb was there with the Mississippi State coach, who was sizing me up in my school clothes. He introduced himself and reached out to shake my hand. After the usual pleasantries, we sat down, and the coach started into his sales pitch.

"We've watched you a little bit," he said, "and we like what we've seen on film. We like your playing style. We like your size. Now, I know you play running back here in high school, but I was wondering if you would be willing to play fullback at the college level?"

"No, sir," I said.

Coach Grubb's eyes got wide, as if to say, *Are you serious, Matt?! This is Mississippi State! An SEC school!*

The visiting coach also appeared stunned. He was probably used to hearing kids say they would do anything to play at his school.

Finally, I broke the awkward silence by asking, "Is that it?"

The coach nodded, and I stood up to return to class.

I understood the coach's interest in changing my position, because I was more athletic than the typical fullback. Playing me at fullback probably would have made sense for Mississippi State, but it didn't make sense for me because of the purpose I found in carrying the ball.

The recruiting process was much simpler when I was coming up than it is for high school athletes today. The number of recruiting websites, evaluators, and rankings seems to have grown exponentially. Reporting on recruiting has become a business. Social media has created direct access between the high school athletes being recruited and the (often overzealous) supporters of colleges who want those kids to go to their favorite school. All the attention on recruits today has helped high school kids get their game film in front of more schools and coaches. But it has also brought the potential dangers of being in the spotlight to—let's keep in mind—teenagers.

When asked what I would say to young athletes going through the recruiting process today, I advise that they hold loosely all the attention they receive. It would be easy for them to base their identity or sense of value on what they're being told about their football abilities. It's important to recognize that most of the people doling out the praise do not even know them. Those people just want to get the best recruits they can on their campus and then let them compete against each other to see who actually gets to play.

With all the attention they receive, too many kids go into the recruiting process with the expectation that their favorite school will offer them a scholarship. That's only setting themselves up for disappointment. That stack of recruiting letters doesn't guarantee a single scholarship offer. Then the kid who has built his self-worth on all the attention he's been getting winds up embarrassed on National Signing Day when there is no offer on the table to sign. That's why I say hold all that attention loosely.

The truth is, all it takes is one school to believe in you enough to offer you the opportunity to play in college. Even then, high school athletes must have a plan for what they want to accomplish as student-athletes, and then work hard to make the most of the opportunities they're given. They need to enter college sports with their minds open to the possibility (which is really more of a *probability* for most athletes) that their college experience might actually set them up for a different path in life than expected.

According to one study, only 1.6 percent of college football players make it to the NFL. And then, as I mentioned earlier, the average length of an NFL career is only 3.3 seasons. College football—and the educational opportunities that come with it—should be viewed as a stepping stone to the next path in life. It allows time for student-athletes to develop an additional passion beyond their passion for football. Pursuing that second passion will last much, much longer than sports.

I don't play the what-if game about my recruiting experience. I don't wonder what might have happened if my game film had made it to college coaches before my senior year. I don't wonder what might have happened if I had played at a school better known for football success. I don't wonder what might have happened if one of the big schools had offered me a scholarship.

I received two offers to play college football—from Tulane and McNeese State. Neither was a big school, and only Tulane played in Division I-A. I had been on their campus a few times with my dad, but I didn't take an official recruiting visit until after I had already committed to sign there. A couple of their coaches visited me at school during lunch one day. Heads turned when they entered the cafeteria because one of the coaches was wearing a black coat that made him look like a member of the Mafia. I never spoke to the running backs coach during the recruiting process. I don't remember ever hearing a recruiting pitch about whether they thought I could play as a freshman. With no other I-A offers, I didn't need a sales pitch. I believe God opened the door for me at Tulane, and I could not have scripted a better plan than the one He had for me there.

I love Tulane. I appreciated my time there, and I stay connected to the football program as a proud alum. But during my time at Tulane, building a strong football program was not a top university priority. We didn't have our own stadium; we played in the Superdome, the home of the New Orleans Saints. We didn't draw many fans to our games, and rightfully so, because we were not winning conference championships and going to bowl games every year. Tulane was not where I had hoped to play, because I thought bigger schools and programs would offer me more, but I was prepared to make the most of the opportunity I was being given.

My prayer while I was being recruited was that I would receive a football scholarship and that the decision on which school to attend would be clear and come easily for me. I believe that my receiving just one Division I-A offer was God's way of answering that prayer. What could be easier than deciding to accept the only offer available?

Going to Tulane meant I would be attending school only thirty minutes from home. My parents could attend every home game. And as it turned out, Tulane prepared me well for playing in the NFL.

My four years with the Green Wave ended up being a time when God would continually prove that if I remained committed to His way and obedient to His Word, He would do more than I could have hoped for or imagined with what I considered *less*.

The Best Days

I loved high school football. The practices, the weight room, the workouts, being around my teammates, the bus rides to games, and the bus rides home. Between college and the NFL, I played fourteen seasons after my high school career ended, and I can still look back and say that high school football was the last time I was able to play for the sheer love of the game. In college, football was starting to become more like a business for me. In the NFL, football *is* a business. And the game was my job.

Occasionally, memories come to mind of a high school teammate saying something funny in the huddle that made everyone laugh. Or teammates poking fun at each other during practice. Or somebody saying something silly at the bottom of a pile, in the middle of a game, surrounded by teammates and players from the other team, that made you think, *Where did* that *come from?* I built lasting relationships in high school. When I go back to Slidell, some of my old teammates and I get the crew back together to relive some of the best days of our lives.

I appreciated coaches like Wayne Grubb, Artie Liuzza, and Greg Varnado, who modeled hard work, instilled discipline in us, and held us to high expectations that forced us players to step up our game. We were coached by good men who became coaches not only for the love of sports but also to help boys develop into young men.

I loved everything about high school football.

5

STARTING ALL OVER

During high school, I developed a summer routine of riding my bicycle to our high school stadium for workouts. Summers in Slidell were hot and sticky. A typical day had a high temperature over 90 degrees with humidity over 90 percent. "Take some water," my dad would always remind me when I left the house.

I would be the only person at the field during those days. My workout consisted of running stadiums—up and down the rows of bleachers—and then going onto the field and running through plays with imaginary defenders to evade. Once I broke into the open field, I would run sixty to eighty yards for conditioning.

When Bryan was preparing to play at McNeese State, he started working summers at the same port in Lake Charles where my dad had worked. We had uncles who still worked there, and Bryan would tell me on the phone that throwing the 110-pound bags was difficult but that I could handle it. I decided that when I turned eighteen, I would stay with Bryan to work with him and our uncles as a test to see if I was as tough as Dad.

Before reporting to Tulane, I moved in with Bryan for a few weeks and got picked up on a crew with him. We would go into the bottom of a cargo ship at night and fill it with bags of rice, corn, and flour that we took off of pallets. Bryan taught me how to stack the bags properly and how to grab and throw them so they would land where we wanted them and we wouldn't have to spend extra time and precious energy adjusting the stacks. A pallet usually held fourteen bags, and we each threw seven. The crane operator kept dropping in more pallets whether we were caught up or not. There was no time for relaxing and no room for fatigue at the bottom of a ship.

After I caught on to throwing the bags, Bryan told me, "Look, we've got an eight-hour shift in here. But if we don't stop to take a break, we can get this done in five and a half hours and get paid for eight." I was all for that, so Bryan and I hammered out the work without taking breaks. In another lesson on the benefits of working hard, we were able to pick up overtime work at double pay. I liked that!

Bryan and I made for a good team, and we experienced together the work we had heard our dad talk about while we were growing up.

Thanks to the port work, I reported to Tulane a little stronger than after my typical summer workouts, and I walked immediately into a competitive situation.

Every starter from the offensive line returned for the 2004 season, but the coaching staff had big questions to answer in the backfield. Quarterback J. P. Losman and running back Mewelde Moore had been drafted into the NFL. Mewelde had started all four years and left as the school's all-time leading rusher. Jovon Jackson, a junior, had the inside track on taking over the lead running back spot based on his performance after Mewelde missed the final three games of the previous season with an injury. A month before the first game, head coach Chris Scelfo told the media that the job was Jovon's to lose. Ray Boudreaux was also back as a redshirt freshman.

I was one of three incoming running backs, and the others—Ryan Bewley and Ade Tuyo—came from large high schools in Texas.

Tulane's coaches seemed genuinely excited when I gave them my oral commitment to attend their school. I thought maybe they knew they were getting a real steal in me. Soon after reporting for practice, I started to wonder if I had misread their feelings. My recruiting class included players from a handful of southeastern states, such as Georgia, Florida, and North Carolina. On my first trip to campus, I learned that some recruits had already started attending classes and had received help finding a place to stay and a summer job before our camp began. No one had told me that kind of help was available.

I drove each day from Slidell into New Orleans for the daily workouts, making a commute similar to Dad's during his thirty-six years working with Shell. I didn't own a car, so I drove my mom's Honda Accord, which my parents eventually gave me. The drive was a little over thirty miles one way, over the original Twin Span, a pair of bridges more than five miles long that cross Lake Pontchartrain. I stayed on campus all day. We worked out in the morning, watched film, and spent time learning the playbook. I hung out a little to get to know my teammates before heading back home for the night. When I was dog tired from the day, the drive home wasn't much fun, especially with traffic mixed in. On Saturdays, I went to the high school to run stadiums and run through Tulane's plays on my own. Sunday was a day for church and relaxing with my family.

I already realized that I faced some stiff competition to get playing time as a freshman, and then one day an offensive coach walked up to me and started talking about how good the other two running back recruits were. I didn't know what motivated him to say that, but I wanted to tell him, "Hey, I'm here to compete too."

One night at home, I updated my dad on the challenge ahead of me. His response seemed to be an effort to prepare me for the possibility that the coaches might redshirt me that season. If the coaches redshirted me, I wouldn't play in games that season but I also wouldn't lose one of the four seasons I could play under NCAA rules.

"I'm not redshirting," I said.

"Redshirting isn't a bad thing," he said, "because you would get time to acclimate to college football, and you'd still get to work out and practice. But you'd get another year to play."

With the same determination I'd had when I spoke to my dad in the car after my first practice as a seven-year-old, I firmly informed him, "I'm not redshirting. I'm gonna play."

The summer leading into camp was exciting because I was getting my first taste of taking the next step up in football. I quickly saw the physical difference between me and the juniors and seniors. There's a big gap between being eighteen years old and twenty-one or twenty-two. There were some grown men in our locker room! I was fresh out of high school and still developing physically. In addition to being fully grown, they had spent three or four years in a college weight room.

I knew I needed to step up my training, but I had no doubt I could compete with these guys. Seeing the physical challenge inspired me.

Making a Name for Myself

As camp opened, I figured I was the last running back on the depth chart.

When the equipment managers handed out helmets and pads, they stuck a piece of tape on the front of our helmets with our last name handwritten on it. With almost a hundred players in full gear on the practice field, including many new guys, it takes time for coaches to learn who the players are.

Having the handwritten "FORTE" on my helmet served as a

reminder that once you sign with a program and are out of the recruiting process and all the attention and hype it brings, the coaches still need to get to know you.

I turned that into a positive. I knew how to get the coaches to know my name: Let them see number 25 running down the field on every snap because I'm making plays. My high school accomplishments no longer mattered. This was a new level of football with new coaches and new teammates. I was back to square one.

Ever since I started playing football, whenever I made a mistake, I made a mental note of what I did wrong, and the next time that situation arose, I capitalized on my experience to not repeat the mistake. That served me well heading into my first season of college football with so much to prove.

I didn't catch many passes in high school because we ran the ball most of the time. And when I did catch passes, they were usually short throws, like screen passes. In my first practices at Tulane, I learned that passes came out of the quarterback's hand faster and with more mustard on them than in high school. For the first time, I heard the whistle of the ball spiraling through the air as it zipped toward my hands.

I didn't wear gloves in high school, but I started wearing them at Tulane to help me catch the ball and to keep my hands from getting beat up while blocking defenders.

Greg Davis Jr., our running backs coach, cited Mewelde Moore as an example of the do-it-all type of running back that NFL coaches looked for. Wanting to become an every-down back, I worked on my receiving by catching hundreds of passes off a JUGS machine—equipment we didn't have in high school. I caught passes thrown by the machine to my right and left and at various angles. Quarterbacks stayed after practices to get extra reps throwing, and I stayed with them to sharpen my route running and catch live balls. My goal was to go through a practice without a single dropped pass.

An every-down back needs to be in peak condition. When a player on the field gets tired and needs a breather, he taps his helmet to let the coaches know to send in a replacement. I didn't just want to be an every-down back; I was determined to never tap out. So I ran extra to build my endurance.

Coach Davis had been on staff at Texas in 1998, the year Longhorns running back Ricky Williams won the Heisman Trophy as the best player in college football. Ricky also played minor-league baseball. Coach told me that Ricky returned to football practice a bit heavier because he didn't run as much in baseball. Ricky was a big guy anyway, so to work back into football shape, he ran all the way to the end zone every time he ran the ball in practice, and then he jogged back to the huddle.

During run periods, when we worked on the run offense and defense, a back typically continued ten or fifteen yards downfield after breaking through the line. Just as Coach had described Ricky's habit for me, I ran farther, going forty or fifty yards, and then—instead of tapping my helmet—I ran back to the huddle. If I wanted to stay on the field in games, I needed to stay on the field in practice, too.

Not in Slidell Anymore

Off the field, I experienced how different life was living in a dorm rather than at home.

I will not say my roommate's name, but he played on defense and didn't seem to take football seriously. When classes started, he seemed to be skipping classes. It turned out he was dealing with mental health issues.

Our dorm room had two twin beds with desks in between. I blocked off my area in the middle because I didn't know what to make of this guy. He would wake me up coming in at four or five o'clock in the morning, and I would tell him, "Dude, we have to get up soon for workouts." He didn't seem to care.

One night, I woke up to him talking loudly. I rolled over and saw him sitting on his bed, talking on the phone. Based on his side of the conversation, I thought he might have called a suicide hotline. Then he said into the phone, "I'm thinking about killing myself."

Trying not to draw attention to myself and reveal that I had heard him, I looked to see whether he had a gun. I didn't see one. Within minutes, I heard a knock on our door. My roommate answered and walked out with whoever had come to see him. The next day, when I came back from practice, all his belongings had been removed. I never saw or heard from him again.

We weren't using the word *adulting* back then, but it didn't take me long to realize that being on my own at college was entirely different than the security I enjoyed in my parents' home.

During summer workouts, I had connected with Mike Parenton, a freshman offensive lineman from Thibodaux, Louisiana. One of the first things I noticed about Mike were his Air Jordan cleats. Offensive linemen typically don't have swag like Jordan cleats. That look was more for skill players. I was too curious not to ask about his Jordans.

"Yeah, bruh, I'm jaywalking," he said.

I was like, *Okay. This guy's interesting.*

Mike kind of latched onto me, I guess because we were both freshmen trying to figure out the transition to college football. After that initial conversation, practically every time Mike saw me, he'd say, "I'm jaywalking, bruh." I tried to avoid him because I didn't want to hear the same silly joke over and over. Plus, Mike tended to talk a lot.

When we were being assigned roommates, I thought to myself, *Please don't let it be this dude.* Instead, I was assigned the defensive player who ended up leaving.

Mike's roommate was a nonathlete, and Mike would complain about having a regular student for a roommate because he stayed out late and woke Mike up when he came into the room. Mike wanted a football roommate with the same daily schedule as his. He also said that having a football buddy for a roommate would allow the two to lean on each other as they went through their freshman year.

After my first roommate left, I got to know Mike better and liked him. He was a brilliant guy and a lot of fun, except for the jaywalking joke. I told Mike I had a room to myself and suggested he ask the RA if he could move into my room. The RA permitted him to make the switch, and Mike became not only my roommate but also my best friend in college. We roomed together all four years at Tulane, and he opened plenty of holes for me to run through on the field.

Mike signed with the New York Jets after Tulane and spent one season there. Since 2012, he has worked with the New Orleans Saints and is now their vice president of pro personnel. When I had a shoe contract with Nike, I kept Mike supplied with Jordans, and he would tell me how impressed the Saints players were with his shoes. And yes, he still sometimes tells me he's "jaywalking." Now, though, we both laugh.

Earning My Place

The guys at the bottom of the depth chart are assigned to scout team duty during practice—just like during my freshman and sophomore years in high school when I ran scout team to help prepare our varsity starters for the next opponent. As I did in high school, I turned scout team work into an opportunity at Tulane. I wanted to make the defense look bad to show my coaches and teammates what I could do.

Fortunately, most of the time, a player can overcome a lack of college experience and recruiting stars by continually making plays in practice. So that's what I did. Day by day, I began earning more respect during practice. I felt like I was working my way up the depth chart that would be released for the first time before our first game.

The fruit of my hard work showed up when we started intrasquad scrimmages during practice. In our first scrimmage, I made a nice one-handed catch of a pass. In our next scrimmage, Jovon and I split the bulk of the work in the backfield.

While I warmed up for a later scrimmage, I spotted my parents in the stands. I didn't need extra motivation that day, but knowing that Mom and Dad were there watching fired me up. During that scrimmage, I caught a screen pass and turned it into a sixty-yard touchdown. Our senior safety had an angle on me on that play as I raced downfield, but I still outran him to the end zone.

"Hey, you said it," Dad told me after practice. "You're not going to redshirt. You're going to make them put you on the field."

When the coaches showed us the film of that scrimmage and came to my touchdown, they backed up the film to watch it again. I saw some of the coaches looking at each other. That was how I would make them put me on the field.

Heading into our first game, the coaches asked to meet with Jovon and me.

"Y'all have both earned the right to play," one of the coaches told us. "So we're going to split time between you. Jovon, you'll get your series and drives, and Matt, you'll get yours."

I had risen from the depths of the depth chart to become an integral part of our offense.

Through the first seven weeks of the season, Jovon had about twice as many carries as I did. Behind our veteran offensive line, he was running well, including a couple of 100-yard games. In our eighth game, against Navy, I rushed for 82 yards on seventeen carries, the most I'd had to that point in the season. I also caught three passes for 27 yards and a touchdown.

The following week, ahead of our game against Army, my big chance came when Jovon injured his hamstring. No player, no matter how much he desires a greater role, wants to see a teammate get hurt. But injuries are a part of football, and you must always be ready to step in when called, regardless of the reason.

Coach Davis told me that week, "We're not splitting time anymore. You've got to play every down."

I shifted into full preparation mode for getting the ball on almost every play by running to the end zone on every carry in practice and then running back to the rest of the offense. The risk was that I would wear myself out before the game, but I would not be unprepared to carry a full load on Saturday.

It was a good thing, too, because the coaches put the ball in my hands a lot against Army in the Superdome. I was ready. But no one was prepared for us to lose our starting quarterback, Lester Ricard, to a broken wrist early in the second half. His injury made it even more crucial that we run the ball well.

We won 45–31, and I ended the game with thirty-four carries for 216 yards and three touchdowns. I also caught three passes for 67 yards and another score. In my first collegiate start, my 216 rushing yards were the fourth-most in a game in school history.

Jovon only missed the Army game with his hamstring injury, but even after he came back he was limited, leaving me as the featured back for two difficult games to end the season: at TCU and at home against Louisville, the seventh-ranked team in the nation. TCU was geared up to stop the run with our backup quarterback, Richard Irvin, starting. I had to work hard to find running room in rushing for 97 yards on twenty-eight carries, and I also caught four passes for 38 yards. Richard, though, played an awesome game. TCU's focus on our running game opened the field for him to throw five touchdown passes, and we won 35–31.

We went into the Louisville game—which had been rescheduled from September because of Hurricane Ivan—looking for our fourth consecutive victory. A win would also have qualified us for a postseason bowl game. That game was a rough one, though, with Louisville beating us pretty easily, 55–7. Our offense struggled the entire game, and I finished with 70 yards on seventeen carries and three receptions for 15 yards.

Jovon and I both finished the season rushing for 624 yards.

My freshman season provided further evidence of what I had learned as a kid: Hard work pays off. I knew from age seven that I had talent. Even though I worked hard throughout my high school career, I had never put in the level of work I did in transitioning into college football. I learned workouts I had never heard of, like running conditioning drills carrying a football filled with water to make it heavier. I had started the season splitting time with a more experienced teammate and ended the season as our workhorse.

Even though there was a point when—as my dad pointed out—I faced the possibility of redshirting the season, I never doubted that I belonged at Tulane. I learned that what separated schools like Tulane from the big schools I had hoped would offer me a chance to play was not the players in the skill positions. The main difference I noticed was the size of the offensive and defensive linemen.

I had also navigated the transition from high school to being a college student living away from home for the first time. I was surprised by the challenge of being a student-athlete in college. Tulane took academics seriously. We were not one of those schools where football players didn't have to go to class. In fact, Tulane's requirements for athletes to maintain their eligibility were stricter than the NCAA's. But nobody would wake us up on time or drag us to class. We had to be dedicated to football *and* academics.

We worked out at five o'clock in the morning, attended classes, and then practiced and watched film. Sometimes, I needed to take a night class to keep a full schedule. Being a student-athlete was a full-time-plus job.

College football also felt more serious than in high school. I still played football for the love of the game, but there was an understanding that because we were on scholarship, because we were receiving a free education and free meals, the school had invested money in us to play there. It was not Monopoly money, either. We needed to produce results on the field and represent Tulane well on and off the field.

The transition to being a college student-athlete was one of the most difficult challenges I have faced in my life. Some of the freshmen from my signing class were not up to the challenge. I was surprised by how many didn't return after that first season. They chose to walk away from their scholarships and a free education because the work no longer seemed worth it. I embraced the challenge because of the aspirations I chased.

But I never could have anticipated the adversity our team would face the following season.

6

THE KATRINA SEASON

For the first nineteen years of my life, living along the Louisiana Gulf Coast, my family had never had to evacuate because of a hurricane. For some hurricanes we were prepared to leave Slidell, but the storm veered off each time toward Texas or Mississippi or didn't develop as much as the forecasters had projected.

Then came Hurricane Katrina.

Heading into the 2005 preseason camp, my optimism was high for the upcoming season. I liked the number of experienced players we had returning, and personally I still felt the momentum from the three-game stretch that had ended the previous season. The Army game was huge, of course, and then we had defeated TCU. Even though Louisville took it to us in our final game, I enjoyed playing against a top-ten team and believed the experience would help me going forward.

Jovon Jackson was back as well, and his hamstring was fully recovered. Even though Jovon was a senior, the coaches named me the starter in our time-split because of my performances during spring practices. Preparations for our first game, against rival Southern Miss—a rare Sunday game—were going well. Everything was trending toward a memorable season.

Then, on August 25, ten days before the Southern Miss game, Katrina hit Florida as a Category 1 hurricane. It was downgraded to a tropical storm as it crossed the peninsula and entered the Gulf of Mexico. I didn't pay much attention to the hurricane because the forecasts called for it to turn north toward the Florida Panhandle. Classes hadn't started yet, and our team spent part of the next day, a Friday, participating in an annual community service event by helping students move into their dorms. We held regular practices on Friday and Saturday.

Meanwhile, Katrina exploded as it moved across the Gulf of Mexico, and the forecasts changed to predict landfall on the Mississippi and Alabama coasts. On Saturday, mandatory evacuations were ordered for our region of Louisiana. Our campus was closed, and students were instructed to evacuate.

On Sunday morning, Katrina reached Category 5 status. The football and soccer teams had been told that we would be bused out of New Orleans at 12:30 p.m. to Jackson State University in Jackson, Mississippi. But that morning, as Katrina continued to intensify, our departure was moved up to 10:30 a.m. We had all packed for a week because our first game wouldn't be until Sunday, September 4, in Hattiesburg, Mississippi. We expected to return home immediately after the game.

Having never experienced an evacuation, I was shocked at the traffic on our way out of town. Jackson should have been about a four-hour drive. Instead, it took ten hours.

At Jackson State, we were ushered into the gymnasium, our

temporary home. Our beds for the night were twin-size mattresses with no sheets or pillows. During the evening, we huddled around a small television, trying to determine how bad the hurricane was. A bunch of us were from southern Louisiana, so we tried to stay in touch with our families back home. But my cell phone died before I could get through to my family. Without a pillow, I propped my head on a shoe to sleep.

Monday morning, we awoke to rain and high winds as the edges of the hurricane approached Jackson. Cell phones were starting to run out of juice, and we didn't have enough electrical outlets for everyone to charge their phones. I charged mine enough to call my parents, but many of my teammates didn't know whether their families were okay.

In the afternoon, the electricity went off, and cell service was next to nothing. That's when things got a little scary. I didn't know whether the storm would extend as far west as Lake Charles, where my parents and Bryan were staying with family, but it was such a big storm that all of southern Louisiana would likely be hit hard.

We had another workout in the gym on Monday, with the only available light coming from outside. With no electricity, we had no air conditioning and nothing much else to do. That night, I couldn't fall asleep. I lay on my mattress, with my head on my shoe, looking up at the gym ceiling, uncertain what was happening around us and wondering what would happen next. During the middle of the night, a fire alarm went off, startling us awake and sending us outside into the rain until the alarm was determined to be false.

On Tuesday, a few people managed to get cell phone calls to go through. The little bit of information we received was that the damage in New Orleans was worse than we could imagine. That afternoon, our coaches told us that the Southern Miss game had been postponed but we could not go back to New Orleans. With power out all across Jackson, we also could not remain there.

Tulane's athletic officials worked with the leadership of Conference USA and other schools in the conference to find alternatives. The decision was made to send our football team to Dallas, while the soccer teams left for Alabama, where they were scheduled to play in a tournament. When the buses showed up to take us to Dallas, we climbed aboard for the eight-hour trip—at least we hoped it wouldn't be any longer. During a rest stop somewhere in northern Louisiana, we began seeing the damage back home for the first time, via the internet. It truly was more than we could imagine. Entire neighborhoods were flooded. We read stories of people on the rooftops of their homes hoping to be rescued. The death toll was as yet undetermined, but early reports painted a bleak picture.

Our buses arrived in Dallas early Wednesday morning, and we checked into a DoubleTree hotel. There, many of our players were able to make contact with their families for the first time. My family was still safe, but we had two inches of standing water inside our home. Talking with my parents and hearing how unshaken my dad sounded brought a sense of relief and confidence that they would be all right. My parents had a lot of work ahead of them—tearing out carpet, trying to salvage furniture, spraying for mold, and replacing drywall—but compared to stories I was hearing from teammates and coaches whose families had suffered far worse damage, it felt like our family had caught a break. Meanwhile, there were a few players who were still unable to reach their family members.

In Search of Normal

Our first couple of days in Dallas were like living in a fog. The TV news said the situation back home was growing worse. New Orleans looked like a completely different world than I had grown up in. Familiar landmarks that I had taken for granted after driving past them for years were now underwater or gone. Fortunately, everyone on the team had eventually made contact with their relatives.

Our football workouts were as close to normal as we could make them. We practiced at a local high school, and the Dallas Cowboys donated equipment to us. People and groups we didn't know collected clothes and toiletries for us. Restaurants offered us free meals. Our team became part of a national story. SMU and the city of Dallas were exceptionally kind to us.

On Friday, September 2—two days before what was supposed to be the kickoff of an exciting season—the university president announced the cancellation of the fall semester. But he added that the sports teams would continue their seasons as a way of representing the university.

But how and where? Our campus was unavailable. The Superdome—where both we and the Saints played home games—had suffered damage, and it was uncertain whether the stadium could be used. (The Saints wound up playing all road games that season.) We were two teams without a home.

In what must be considered a logistical miracle, Tulane's athletic leadership found temporary homes and school arrangements for most of our sports teams. Some relocated to other universities, such as SMU, Texas A&M, and Texas Tech. Our football team—along with a portion of the women's track and field team—relocated to Louisiana Tech in Ruston, Louisiana.

We traveled to Ruston on September 9 to enroll in classes there and move into our home for the semester—an empty dorm that was set to be demolished. The locks and chains that had been cut to open the doors were still on the ground when we arrived. We shared the lower floors of the dorm with families who had been displaced by Katrina. We were grateful to have a longer-term place to stay and still have a football season, and we recognized what Louisiana Tech had done to make us as comfortable as possible. We were told that Tech's football players had carried mattresses into the dorm for us to sleep on. Tech students gave us new linens and towels. And, if nothing else, seeing the displaced families in our dorms provided daily perspective of how good we still had it.

But I also want to try to represent the adversity our team faced that season.

Staying at Louisiana Tech brought stability, but our day-to-day experience was nothing that any other Division I-A football program had to endure. Not surprisingly, when unforeseen circumstances caused a soon-to-be-demolished dorm to be reopened, some features and functions didn't operate normally. My room was on the eighth floor, and I called the elevator a death trap because of how many times our guys got stuck inside and missed class waiting for help to arrive. Walking eight flights of stairs numerous times per day reminded me not to complain about life's smaller inconveniences.

Tech shared their practice fields with us, which meant we had to work around their schedule and practice wherever and whenever we could. Sometimes we practiced on open fields that were worn and dusty. The basketball arena housed our coaches' offices and film room. We had a makeshift weight room that was barely adequate. Our locker room was a large open space with folding chairs. Our travel bags, which we packed our equipment into for road games, also served as our lockers. Even a normal locker room must be kept super-sanitized, and several players contracted staph infections because of our setup.

College athletic programs preach proper nutrition to athletes, but providing us with healthier food wasn't possible at Tech. We ate in the regular dining hall, munching on cold pizza and nachos with liquid cheese. We often practiced at night because Tech's team had priority on its facilities—and rightly so. But Ruston, a small city of about 20,000 people, seemed to shut down early. We were hungry after every practice, and evening workouts forced us to rush into town afterward to try to make it to Subway or some other fast-food joint before it closed. Staying at my preferred playing weight wasn't easy that season.

Making a Decision

As it turned out, we opened our season two weeks later than planned. The Southern Miss game was pushed back to November at the end of the regular season. Our new opener was supposed to be a home game against Mississippi State. Instead, we played in Shreveport, Louisiana, and lost 21–14 in a game that was tied in the fourth quarter.

In one sense, I was thankful just to be able to play the game; and despite all the upheaval, it was a game we could have won. Leading up to the game, Coach Scelfo talked to us about keeping our perspective amid adversity, highlighting the importance of playing the game for the students of Tulane and the people of New Orleans. Still, when we stepped between the lines, none of that mattered for the next sixty minutes on the game clock. We played the game to win, and we didn't.

We returned to Dallas a week later to play SMU and won that game 31–10. Game time was moved up a few hours because of Hurricane Rita. We were prepared to stay overnight in Dallas and sleep on SMU's gym floor in case the storm caused problems for the bus ride back to Ruston. Fortunately, we were able to return without incident that night.

The following week was our "homecoming" game against Southeastern Louisiana, at LSU's Tiger Stadium in Baton Rouge. In the aftermath of Rita, all the hotels in and around Baton Rouge were full. That led to our first trip back into New Orleans, where we spent the night before the game sleeping on air mattresses in a country club banquet room. The country club was on the city's east side, so we drove through the heart of New Orleans to get there. Everyone on the bus sat in stunned silence as we got our first glimpse of the city almost six weeks after Katrina hit. It felt like driving into a war zone, seeing military equipment and personnel everywhere enforcing curfews and providing security.

We typically wore green jerseys for home games, and we were the home team against Southeastern; but when we had left for Jackson the week before the season started, we had taken only our white jerseys with us. So we wore white for every game.

We defeated Southeastern Louisiana, 28–21, to improve to 2–1. But then we didn't win again, dropping our final eight games to finish at 2–9.

As the losses mounted, I sensed more guys starting to pack it in. That happens on some teams when players become accustomed to losing. This wasn't a case of players with bad attitudes bringing down the rest of the team. We had legitimate reasons for not playing our best. Our resources were limited. We had a tiny weight room and went head-to-head each weekend with opposing players who had worked out all week in a Division I-A–level weight room. We had lost our home field advantage for half the games. Over an eleven-week span, we played eleven games in eleven cities and stadiums. We had to make a five-hour bus trip to Houston on the day of the game instead of traveling the day before. Another hurricane—Wilma—led to a game in Florida being played a day earlier than scheduled. Another time, a last-minute change in our travel plans, due to a mix-up by our charter operator, caused us to leave a day early for a "home" game in Alabama.

In a sport where routines lead to optimal performance, we never had a normal week.

I felt bad for our seniors—especially for the majority who wouldn't go on to play in the NFL. I could only imagine how it felt to see their football careers end in this fashion. Senior Day—their day to be honored for their commitment to Tulane football and the university—occurred in Monroe, Louisiana, three hundred miles from our campus.

At least we were able to play an entire season. Some of the other Tulane teams had their seasons canceled.

Just getting through the season was an accomplishment. After it was over, our team received two national sports awards, recognizing the courage and spirit we displayed. In 2015, ten years after Katrina, Tulane took the unusual step of inducting all 308 student-athletes from the 2005–2006 school year into the Tulane Hall of Fame.

I understood why some players lost hope during our season. I didn't blame them. That season was hard. But I chose to keep my positivity through the adversity.

Going back to my first practice at age seven, when I got knocked down, I didn't make an excuse; I made a decision. I decided to get back on my feet and figure out what I needed to do better the next time.

When we make those types of decisions, tough times produce the most growth. A common reaction to tough times is to chase our emotions, taking action based on how we feel. That's a natural response. But in most cases, the more beneficial decision is to do the opposite of what feels natural. Here's what makes that difficult: Self-pity, excuses, and complaints pacify our emotions in the moment. The benefits of not making excuses, not complaining, and not feeling sorry for ourselves come later. Often, much later.

The decision I am referring to, ultimately, is a decision between reacting to our feelings *now* or setting aside those feelings in favor of growing later. Stated that way, the correct decision seems obvious. But it requires working against human nature.

The 2005 season was a nightmare in many ways, but I stayed committed to my dream of playing in the NFL. My statistics that year weren't great—655 yards and four rushing touchdowns, twenty-three receptions for 163 yards and a score. You don't expect great stats playing for a 2–9 team. Still, I didn't complain, because complaining only expends energy and doesn't solve the problem. Instead, I decided to grow through the adversity, both as a person and as a player. And eventually the growth did come.

7

A SEASON OF TRANSITIONS

The Tulane campus reopened for the spring 2006 semester, but Katrina had caused an estimated $200 million in damage, and construction work was underway across the campus. Faculty members and staff had been laid off because of spending cuts from the economic loss, and about half the school's athletics programs were suspended for financial reasons. The university's recovery would be slow and painful.

Spring practices were delayed until April while a new artificial surface was installed on our practice fields. We moved into a refurbished locker room that had been under four feet of water four months earlier. Our weight room was also in the middle of a makeover, with new equipment still arriving. We operated with an odd mix of trying to return to normal and a bunch of new thrown in.

During the spring semester and into the summer, my mindset

was one of realizing that time was running out for what I wanted to accomplish. I was a junior and twenty years old. I was no longer a teenager. My feelings reminded me of the end of my junior year in high school, when only Tulane had watched me play and I was wondering whether I would receive a football scholarship offer. Going into my junior year now, I knew I needed to have a good season, a breakout season perhaps, with statistics that would get the attention of NFL scouts. If I didn't, my NFL aspirations might never advance beyond the dream stage.

With Jovon having graduated, I was ready to handle the bulk of our carries. And then we opened our season with a dud, falling behind early and losing 45–7 at Houston. We could not get our running game going, although I did contribute by catching a forty-nine-yard touchdown pass among my five receptions for 69 yards.

We bounced back with a big win, going on the road to defeat an SEC opponent, Mississippi State, 32–29. I rushed for 170 yards on twenty-nine carries with a touchdown that gave us a 32–7 lead. Then, after Mississippi State mounted a big comeback, I gained a first down that helped us run out the clock and hold on for the win.

We entered October with a 1–3 record, still struggling to establish a consistent game. But then we began a four-game stretch in which I rushed for more than 100 yards each game. It started with 198 yards against Rice, followed by 147 at UT–El Paso, 117 at Auburn (another SEC opponent and ranked eighth in the nation), and 124 yards against Army. I surpassed 2,000 career rushing yards, moving me into seventh place on Tulane's career rushing yardage list.

With four games remaining in the regular season, we were 3–5 but still in the picture for a bowl invitation if we could finish strong. Also, I was only 202 yards away from 1,000 for the season. My parents flew to Kentucky and then drove to West Virginia for our next game, at Marshall, so they could be there if I reached the milestone. During pregame warm-ups, Marshall fans shouted racist comments at our players that I knew they would not have the guts to say to our faces. So I was extra fired up to make their team pay for their comments.

Marshall jumped on us for two early touchdowns and led 21–0 at the end of the first quarter. One concern with falling that far behind so early was that if we didn't put some points on the board soon, we would need to abandon our running game to try to catch up. Fortunately, we were able to score a touchdown early in the second quarter, and I scored on a one-yard run a few minutes later to pull us within a touchdown at 21–14. The score stayed that way through halftime.

On our first possession of the second half, I loved the play calls: I touched the ball on five of the first six plays—three rushes and two receptions, including a long pass play down the sideline. On the seventh play, the coaches called my number again, and I scored on a four-yard run through the middle of the line to tie the score at 21.

Two possessions later, after our special teams blocked a field goal attempt, I thought we were on a drive that would give us the lead. We had moved the ball into Marshall territory when our quarterback, Lester Ricard, threw a fifteen-yard pass that was intercepted by a linebacker named Josh Johnson. Marshall had scored on a pick-six in the first quarter, and I was not going to watch them score another defensive touchdown. I was in the backfield for pass protection on the play, and I immediately knew I was the only one who could prevent a touchdown. I had a good angle on Johnson and caught up with him around our 30 yard line. I took him to the ground with an ordinary tackle, and instantly the inside of my left knee felt like it caught on fire. I didn't hear a pop or feel the knee buckle—just a burning feeling.

I tried to get to my feet and couldn't. I would never lie on the field unless I was really hurt, and my dad knew that. This was the first time he had seen me stay on the ground since my first carry in practice as a seven-year-old. Our trainers helped me to the sideline and examined my knee.

"It's loose," one of the trainers told me. They said they wanted me to have an MRI scan after we returned home.

We lost the game 41–21.

On the flight home, my knee started swelling more than it already had, even though I was icing it as the trainers instructed. By the time the plane landed, the joint had stiffened to the point where I could barely flex it.

I had never experienced a burning sensation like I did on that tackle, so I had no history for anticipating what the MRI would reveal. I hoped the doctors would tell me I just needed a little rest and that I would be good to go once everything calmed down inside my knee. Instead, I was diagnosed with tears of the lateral meniscus and posterior cruciate ligament (PCL). The PCL runs along the back of the knee and connects the thighbone to the lower leg bone. The lateral meniscus is cartilage that serves as a shock absorber between the thighbone and shinbone. The good news was that I hadn't also injured my anterior cruciate ligament (ACL), which was a bit unusual because the PCL sits behind the ACL. Still, the doctor said I would need surgery, and once he said "surgery," my season was done.

The only other injury I had suffered that knocked me out of a game came during the playoffs of my junior year in high school, when I hurt my ankle in our last game of the season. This was the first time I would have to watch from the sideline as my team played without me. We lost two of our final three games to finish 4–8. In those three games, our offense struggled, producing only sixteen total points. I couldn't help but feel like I was letting my teammates down by not being out there.

As I evaluated my season, I was pleased to have rushed for 859 yards and eight touchdowns. I liked that I had averaged 5.3 yards per carry. I also caught twenty-eight passes for 360 yards and two other touchdowns, giving me more than 1,200 total yards from scrimmage. Coach Davis had told me I needed to become an all-around back, and in my first season as the feature back, I ran and caught the ball well. In one of Coach Scelfo's weekly press conferences during the season, he had pointed out to the media that I had worked on my blocking to the point that they gave me numerous opportunities to protect the quarterback, and I had not allowed a sack.

Everything had been going according to plan until that tackle at Marshall.

Knee Surgery Number One

Following the PCL tear diagnosis—my first significant injury—I had one moment where my NFL hopes and dreams flashed before my eyes. But then my switch flipped to "I wanna go again" mode.

What are you going to do now? I asked myself. *Football players overcome injuries all the time. What about you? Are you going to work hard to get back and do this again next season?*

I determined that I would be back in time for spring football.

Coach Scelfo connected me with Dr. James Andrews, the world-renowned orthopedic surgeon famous for his surgeries on athletes with knee, elbow, and shoulder injuries. I have always appreciated how Coach made certain I would be in good hands.

I flew with my parents to Birmingham, Alabama, to meet with Dr. Andrews. He was such a kind man with a calming, confident presence. I imagine if I had performed as many surgeries as he had, I would be calm and confident too.

Dr. Andrews studied the MRIs and examined my knee.

"You have a lateral meniscus tear," he said. "The good news is that we don't have to clip out the torn cartilage—because you don't grow new cartilage. But if I sew it together, it will heal. We'll need to keep it straight in a brace. You also have a partial tear of the PCL, but it's not a full tear. We don't even do surgery on PCLs anymore, so we'll let that scar. The biggest thing with the rehab is getting that scar tissue broken down to make sure the PCL is mended back together."

Through his explanation, Dr. Andrews passed his confidence to my parents and me.

After the surgery, when Dr. Andrews told me everything had turned out as expected, I was ready to go. He knew my knee would heal, and I knew I would do the hard work necessary to rehab back to 100 percent.

Finding Purpose in Tragedy

Two unexpected news stories from Tulane football made lasting impacts on me, one personally and one in football.

In the week leading up to our final game of the season, we heard reports that a former teammate, Brandon Spincer, had been shot and killed in New Orleans.

Brandon was a junior when I came into the program, and he started four years at linebacker and safety. At the time of his death, he was twenty-four and had two children. After graduating from Tulane, he began working for a nonprofit that helped at-risk kids in New Orleans, the city he'd grown up in. He was shot by his girlfriend's ex-boyfriend.

When I talked earlier about the physical difference between me as a freshman and the older players, Brandon was one of those dudes who I could tell had been working hard in a college weight room program.

When I came into the program, I stuck with my crew and didn't hang out with Brandon and the older players outside of football. He was well-respected in the locker room for how he played and for the drive and determination he brought to the team. He was one of the experienced players I observed and learned from about the business of playing college football. Even though Brandon and I weren't personally close off the field, he was my brother in the locker room, and I felt his loss.

He was so proud to have earned his degree, and he was someone I assumed would use his education to change the trajectory of his life. Then his life got cut short.

Our team attended the funeral, and during the service I could see how much Brandon's family was hurting. I could not imagine what it would be like to have a family member killed by gunshot. A murder is so sudden, so unexpected, so final.

I didn't know how to process Brandon's death. I hadn't known anyone who died in those circumstances, so this was my first real introduction to the fragility of life and how things can change in an instant. In the mere seconds it took one misguided person to make a poor decision, two young kids lost their father for the rest of their lives.

Our society didn't talk as openly about mental health then, and the players were not provided with professionals to help us process the trauma. It took me years to work through Brandon's death.

I don't think football players are positioned to process trauma well. We play a game that requires us to be callous to pain and adversity, and to make quick transitions. There isn't time to process all the transitions that occur during a football game. I could be sitting on the bench while our defense is on the field, and all of a sudden, we force a turnover; and just like that, we're transitioning back to offense, putting our helmets on, and running back onto the field. Lose a fumble? We were coached to forget about it and move on. "Next play," we'd say. A teammate gets injured? "Next man up" was the mentality we were taught.

In life, it's unhealthy to be callous to what is happening to others around us. It's detrimental to transition to the next step without processing what has happened. We need time to assimilate, and we need people to walk through the process with us.

Romans 8:28 is a popular Bible verse to quote: "We know that all things work together for the good of those who love God, who are called according to his purpose." I'm sure I heard someone quote that verse in response to Brandon's death. But what good could come from that?

I'm in my late thirties now, and only recently have I begun to understand the depth of that verse. God doesn't *cause* evil to happen, and He doesn't *want* evil to happen. But evil is a consequence of our fallenness, and the world, as a result, is broken. God has free will to do whatever He wants. If He didn't, He wouldn't be God. Because we are made in His image, He has given us free will as well. Otherwise, we would be robots, incapable of having a relationship with Him. But unlike God, we are sinful creatures. When people do evil things, like the guy who decided to kill Brandon, it isn't that God couldn't step in and prevent the evil from happening. But He gave us free will so that each of us would ultimately decide whether we want to be in relationship with Him or not—to use our lives for good or for evil.

God is both omniscient (all-knowing) and omnipresent, and He works providentially in each of our lives. That's what Romans 8:28 is ultimately getting at. God allows the consequences of our fallen nature and our fallen world to play out in our lives. At any moment, any one of us can choose our own path because of our free will. That's why bad things happen. And yet God is able to work within those events and circumstances to build our character, form us into the likeness of Jesus Christ our Savior, and draw us closer to Himself. In God's overall purpose for our lives, even bad things can ultimately result in something good.

In the aftermath of Brandon's murder, God raised up within me a strong disdain for gun violence. Though I didn't know how or when at the time, I knew that someday I would find a way to fight gun violence to prevent others from being murdered like my teammate.

Setting the Table

A few days after our season ended with a 4–8 record, Coach Scelfo was fired. He had led Tulane's program for eight years, coached more games than any other coach in Tulane history, and was the program's second-winningest coach.

Having my head coach fired was another first for me. I hadn't seen it coming, but I also wasn't shocked. In the first game I missed with my knee injury, our offense was struggling so badly against Southern Miss that Coach opted on one possession to punt on third down. The heat from the media seemed to intensify from that point on. We had also gone four years without a winning record or playing in a bowl game.

Two weeks later, we had our new head coach: Bob Toledo, who had coached at the college level for thirty years, including seven years as head coach of UCLA. Most recently, he had been an assistant at New Mexico, coaching the offense.

Having a new coach sent the players scurrying for any information we could find. For seniors like me, the concern was that the new coach would come in and favor younger players to build for the future. Not so much now as back then, a coach's first year could almost be a free pass on expectations. So why would he invest his time in seniors he would have to replace the next year anyway?

I considered Coach Toledo a big-time coach. I especially liked two things I learned about him. First, he was an offensive-minded coach. Second, he had coached Skip Hicks and DeShaun Foster.

Hicks was a first-team All-America running back at UCLA. He played his junior and senior seasons under Coach Toledo and rushed for 1,000 yards both seasons, then played four years in the NFL. Foster was another great UCLA running back and played all four of his seasons there for Coach Toledo. He rushed for more than 3,000 yards in his collegiate career and went on to play seven seasons in the NFL.

Early in the spring semester, with my rehab on schedule, Coach Toledo asked me to come by his office. When I went in, he said he wanted to watch film with me.

"This is the kind of offense we ran at UCLA," he told me.

He cued up highlights of Hicks and Foster making big runs.

"Look, Matt," he said. "I've watched enough film to know you're the best player on the team. I'm going to give you the ball every play, so I wanted you to be prepared to handle that."

That was all I wanted to hear.

8

UNCOMMON WORK, UNCOMMON RESULTS

Patience.

Football plays are based on timing, and good running backs must have patience to allow their blockers to open holes. Mind you, I'm talking about patience that lasts for maybe a second. During a game when the running game is struggling to get going, we need patience to allow for the game plan to develop or for the play callers to make adjustments. That patience lasts maybe a quarter or two. But the patience required to rehabilitate an injury plays out over months. That patience is essential.

The human body's ability to heal is remarkable. But the body needs time. Being a just-turned-twenty-one-year-old coming off my first surgery and heading into my final opportunity to make good on my NFL aspirations, the idea of patience seemed counterproductive.

The pace of my rehab seemed *so slooooowwwwww.* I spent six

weeks wearing a knee brace and walking to class on crutches. My left quad felt like it was going to fall away from my leg from atrophy. I would look down at my legs and see how much smaller my left calf was than my right one.

Physical therapy started with taking the brace off—relief!—extending my leg, and flexing my toes up and down to begin working my leg muscles. Next, I progressed to the same exercise with a resistance band. *Boring!* I wanted to dig into my Forté work ethic to get back to where I wanted to be faster than the rehab schedule called for. The therapists kept preaching patience. They continually reminded me that all those small movements were building the foundation of my recovery. Slack off on the small movements and I would suffer a setback when the exercises ramped up—and then I'd be starting all over. Attempt to do too much too soon? Same outcome.

I would ask the PTs what else I could be doing to move the healing along at a faster pace.

"You need to let it rest," they said. "You need to let it heal."

Recovering from an injury takes time. The body needs time, and so does the mind, I discovered.

I learned a lot about patience, though not by choice.

The doctors finally gave me a medical clearance to return to the field for spring practices, but only if I wore a knee brace. The brace was bulky and made me feel like I was running with one leg bottled up. My knee felt fine, though, and I tried to convince the trainers I didn't need the brace.

"No, you need it," they insisted. "It's there to protect you."

College teams hold what's called Junior Day during spring practices. Although that season's NFL draft has yet to occur, Junior Day is the opportunity for scouts to start evaluating the next year's draft class. Scouts measure a draft prospect's height and weight, record their time in the forty-yard dash, and grade their game film. Then they take that information back to their organizations, where it is pooled with all the information scouts gather from Junior Days across the country, and the team's talent evaluators assign each prospect a projected round that he is most likely to be drafted in.

I measured at six foot two, 223 pounds going into my senior season. I had the size to play running back in the NFL, but the forty-yard dash time is crucial information for scouts. Forty times get fudged all the time, so scouts want to watch a timed forty in person. Coaches and teammates recommended I not run the forty for scouts since I still had my knee brace and was working my way back into playing shape. But I insisted on running for the scouts. I don't remember my time on Junior Day, but I—and the scouts—knew it was not representative of my speed.

The secondhand reports were that scouts saw me as going either in the seventh and final round of the draft or needing to try to catch on with a team as an undrafted free agent. In essence, I was back to being a two-star recruit hoping to attract a major program.

Doubling Up

To achieve uncommon results, you must do uncommon things. That summer, I decided to double my workouts. Team workouts took place twice a day—a morning shift and an afternoon shift. I chose to participate in both.

In the morning, I lifted weights and ran. I cringe now, remembering the 220s. From the back of one end zone to the far goal line was 110 yards. We ran to that goal line, stopped, turned, and ran 110 yards back. We ran twelve to fifteen of those. Each 220 was timed, and if anyone didn't beat the required time, that 220 didn't count for everyone; and we had to run an extra round to make up for it. Needless to say, it wasn't fun to make the required time and yet have to run again because one of your teammates was too slow. I imagine it wasn't fun being the one who missed the time, either, because everyone who made the time would yell at those who failed.

In addition to conditioning, the timed 220s were about instilling leadership and accountability within the team.

After the first day of morning workouts, I left to work a job that our former quarterback, Lester Ricard, had passed along to me. A Tulane fan hired me to be what I considered a glorified babysitter for his son. I used my time with the boy to mentor him. After spending time with that kid, I came back to campus for the afternoon workout. Our strength and conditioning coach asked me, "What are you doing?"

When I told him I was going to do the second workout, he tried to deter me.

"I don't know what you're trying to do," I said, "but I'm going to work out twice a day."

"All right," he said. "Do your thing."

In the afternoons, I did a different type of lifting than in the morning. I also worked on my injury prevention exercises and drills to strengthen my weaknesses. Then I duplicated the running drills.

Coach Toledo had told me I would get the ball every play, and I trained to run all day on game days.

Record-Setting Farewell

As our preseason march to the season opener neared its end, I felt optimistic about the season. Coach Toledo changed our offense to feature the running game, including more sets with tight ends and a fullback in the I-formation. I had the added benefit that Coach Toledo had retained Coach Davis as our running backs coach, meaning I wouldn't have to get to know a new position coach while learning all the offensive changes.

Coach Toledo viewed me as a team leader, inviting me to be one of the two players from our team to attend Conference USA's annual media day and partake in interviews to preview the season. Also, my name was included on the watch list of candidates for the

Doak Walker Award given after the season to the nation's top running back.

We opened our season with a dud, losing 38–17 at home to Mississippi State. They were more physical than we were, and it showed in our inability to run the ball. I scored on a 39-yard run but rushed for only seven yards the rest of the game. Despite our struggles on the ground, Coach Toledo's commitment to putting the ball in my hands showed in my catching six passes for 49 yards. I also lost a fumble. What I wrote earlier about just forgetting when you fumble? Sure. That sounds good, but running backs never forget their fumbles.

We lost our next game, the conference opener, to Houston, 34–10. But we ran the ball better, and I averaged five yards a carry in rushing for 85 yards. I was active in the passing game again, catching four passes for 22 yards.

Coach Toledo emphasized positivity after our 0–2 start. The game plan going into our next game, against Southeastern Louisiana, was to—in Coach Toledo's words—"pound the rock." And pound it, we did. I finished the game with forty carries for 303 yards and five touchdowns, and we gave Coach his first win at Tulane, 35–27. The 303 rushing yards broke Mewelde Moore's school record by 54 yards. I also broke the Conference USA record for single-game rushing yards. The five rushing touchdowns also broke a school record.

Our schedule didn't allow much time for us to celebrate, because a week later we played the best team we would face all season: second-ranked LSU, which statistically had the top run defense in the nation. We were 40.5-point underdogs. The night before the game, our coaches showed us Tulane's 1981 game against LSU when we trounced the Tigers 48–7. Watching that Tulane team physically handle LSU and keep making plays not only motivated us but also reminded us of the importance of minimizing mistakes.

Against the team that went on to win the national championship that season, we led 9–7 in the first half until LSU kicked a field goal with three seconds left before halftime. I imagine anyone outside our locker room that day was shocked to see us in the game at the half, but that was what we expected. LSU's defense was allowing 26.8 rushing yards *per game* before playing us. Our offensive line was doing a great job, and I had rushed for 37 yards by halftime.

Even midway through the third quarter, we were within one score of LSU. But then we started making mistakes instead of minimizing them. I lost a fumble, and we committed another turnover on an interception. LSU converted both turnovers into touchdowns. Those were mistakes we could not afford to make against the number two team in the country. We ended that game knowing the 34–9 final score didn't tell the whole story. I accounted for 94 yards of offense (73 rushing and 21 receiving). My average of 4.6 yards per carry showed we could effectively run the ball against any opponent on our schedule.

What followed the LSU game is still difficult to explain. We won three of our remaining eight games to finish at 4–8 again, extending the Green Wave's streak of seasons without a bowl appearance to five. But at the same time, I thrived. Coach Toledo kept giving me the ball, to the tune of roughly thirty-four carries per game the rest of the season, during which I rushed for at least 100 yards a game, including a stretch of four consecutive games with over 200 yards rushing (which fell one game shy of the NCAA record). During that streak, I again broke the school and conference single-game rushing records with a 342-yard performance in an overtime victory against SMU.

After my fourth game in a row with at least 200 yards—278 on a season-high forty-four carries against Memphis—our sports information department created the website MattForte25.com with highlights, statistics, and notes to promote my accomplishments to state and national media. The funny thing is, I was not even well-known on the Tulane campus.

A news reporter came to interview me for a story during my hot streak.

"You're leading the NCAA in rushing; you're breaking records," he began. "Do people follow you around campus?"

"No," I told him. "They don't really know me on campus."

To test my claim, the reporter printed my picture from the football media guide and walked around campus, showing students my picture and asking if they could identify me. A few people guessed I was a football player, probably because of the shoulder pads visible in the photo. But the reporter was stunned to learn that even though I was receiving national attention, I was basically unknown at my own school.

I got it. We didn't play our games on campus. We were not having a winning season—again. On campus and in my classes, I was just a regular student; and I was cool with that because I was not getting hounded by people wanting autographs.

I had expected to rush for 1,000 yards for the season, and in my wildest dreams I would reach 1,500. Instead, I finished the season with 2,127 yards and 23 rushing touchdowns. Both set new school single-season records. Nationally, only Kevin Smith of Central Florida gained more rushing yards, with 2,567; and my rushing total was the sixth best in NCAA history. I also was second on our team in receptions, with thirty-two for 282 yards. I had succeeded in becoming an every-down back. My 4,265 career rushing yards placed me second behind Mewelde Moore on Tulane's all-time list by a margin of 99 yards. I also broke the Tulane record for career rushing touchdowns (39) and total touchdowns (44).

After the season, I was selected first-team All-Conference USA and third-team All-America by the Associated Press. I was also named a semifinalist for the Doak Walker and Maxwell awards. Darren McFadden of Arkansas won the Doak Walker Award, and Florida quarterback Tim Tebow received the Maxwell Award as the most outstanding player, in voting by sportswriters and coaches.

Tulane was not the big football school I wanted to play for after high school, but I can look back and see God's providence in making my recruiting decision so simple.

The Tulane portion of my story was a well-lived time of development as a young man. I learned how to be a man out on my own and to rely on myself. I made mature decisions that meant choosing the hard route over the easy way out because I believed those decisions would reap future benefits.

Unfortunately, enduring four losing seasons turned out to prepare me for disappointment in the NFL. From youth leagues through high school, I had only experienced playing on winning teams. That success spoiled me. The tough seasons at Tulane taught me that I was not bigger than the game. The injury in my junior year forced me to grasp how the sport could be ripped from me in just one second. I put in the hard work as my parents taught me, stayed dedicated to the game, and made sacrifices to prepare for an opportunity that might not come to me.

I had accomplished much at Tulane.

And I left with still more to prove.

9

ANSWERING THE QUESTIONS

As my college career wound down, I finally found a group of people trying to out-recruit each other in competition over me: agents!

NCAA rules prohibited players from signing with an agent to represent them in professional football until after playing in their final college game. But nothing stopped agents from making their pitches and securing a verbal commitment.

After I put up back-to-back 200-yard rushing games midway through my senior season and followed that with 342 yards against SMU, it was *game on* for the agents. I guess that was when they decided there might be something to this Forté guy from Tulane after all.

Cell phone calls started coming in from all over, and I had no idea how any of them knew my number. I was not a big cell phone user. I didn't text, and I only used my phone to call my parents, Bryan, my roommate, or a teammate. Call after call started coming in—on my way to class, in class, leaving practice—and I let them all go to voicemail.

"Hi, Matt. This is so-and-so from such-and-such agency, and we see you're having a great season."

"You have a bright future in the NFL, and I want to represent you as your agent."

"Give me a call back so I can talk to you about what our agency can do for you."

I received so many voicemails from agents that I could afford to filter through them and eliminate agents from consideration simply because I didn't like their voice. Those who passed the voice test I asked to mail me a brochure or any other printed materials they had as part of their sales pitch.

I had no help determining what I should look for in an agent. My criteria developed the deeper I moved into the process. From the start, I didn't want to sign with a large agency because I didn't want to be just one of a bunch of guys they represented. But I also didn't want a very small agency because that might mean the agent was inexperienced.

Once I narrowed my choices to three agents, I brought my mom and dad in to meet with each one in person. The funny thing is that my first conversation with the agent I chose was one I did not intend to have.

While I was visiting my parents on a weekend late in my senior season, my phone rang and I answered it without thinking. The caller identified himself as Adisa Bakari, a sports agent from Washington, DC.

Dang! I thought. *I've got to talk to this dude now.*

We wound up having a good conversation. Adisa told me what he believed made him unique as an agent, and then I started asking questions. Who were his current clients? How many draft cycles had he gone through as an agent? Where did he go to school? Had he passed the agents exam with the NFL Players Association? Did he have a law degree? I learned to ask that last question because I wanted an agent with a law degree for handling contracts and business proposals.

Our conversation lasted almost two hours! I kept thinking, *Man, this dude can talk.* But I liked what he was saying, and he seemed to be an agent who was knowledgeable and would genuinely care about me as a person. I liked that his list of clients included skill-position players and defensive backs such as Maurice Jones-Drew of the Jacksonville Jaguars and Antoine Bethea of the Indianapolis Colts. He asked which agents I had talked with and seemed to know how each one worked. He didn't bad-mouth them, but he respectfully compared how he represented his clients to what he knew about the other agents.

The way Adisa described his work was similar to how Dr. Andrews had talked to me about my knee: professional yet personal, confident, and encouraging. Adisa said he invested not only in athletes and their contracts but also in them as people. He told me that even if I made it into the NFL, there was no guarantee how long I would play. He said the NFL would be only a short part of my life, and I needed to use my time in the league to set me up for life beyond football.

I told Adisa about one large agency that was flying my parents and me to meet with their agents in Los Angeles.

"I'm going to tell you how it's going to go," Adisa said. "They're going to fly you out there and wine and dine you, but you're going to be just one of the guys to them. You need to really take a good look at the things they tell you."

The agenda for the trip didn't sound like my style, but I was curious to hear what the agency would offer. My dad was especially looking forward to being taken out to a nice restaurant and put up in an expensive hotel.

After landing in LA, I met the agent who would represent me.

He hadn't attended law school, so I was already thinking this agency would not work out for me. Even the nightlife they treated me to was not my speed. I guess they assumed I would like what they considered fun. As I evaluated the visit during my flight back home, I knew they were not the crew for me.

Then Adisa came to visit my parents and me. He showed up in a full suit. I liked that. He scored more points when, instead of *telling* me how he would represent me to NFL teams, he *showed* me. He had prepared a mock presentation comparing me to Adrian Peterson of the Minnesota Vikings and a couple of the league's other top running backs. His presentation highlighted how my height and build were similar to Adrian's.

Adisa's presentation was compelling. If I were an NFL general manager who sat through the presentation, I would have signed me! Adisa impressed me. Not only that, I liked him. I could see him representing me and being someone I could have a personal relationship with.

So I signed with the agent whose call I didn't intend to answer, and Adisa is still my agent and friend today.

MVP Performance

My parents always emphasized to Bryan and me the importance of a good education.

When our season ended Thanksgiving weekend without our qualifying for a bowl game, I made a business decision. Although I was one semester from completing a bachelor's degree in finance, I decided not to attend school during spring semester in order to focus on improving my draft stock. But I vowed to myself that I would return to Tulane one day to finish my degree.

Adisa had worked his NFL contacts to gather feedback from scouts on my draft prospects. The 2008 draft was shaping up to be deep in running backs, based on juniors who were expected to forego their senior seasons to enter the draft. Adisa said scouts were telling him that because Tulane didn't play in a major conference, my 2,100 rushing yards were not that impressive. The scouts discounted our level of competition. They also questioned my speed. Their reasoning sounded silly. Basically, I had a smooth running style, and they didn't think I looked fast on film—even though, on the film they watched, defenders known to be fast were not catching me. Seriously? That was their takeaway from watching my film?

Adisa and I created a two-step plan to answer those criticisms. First, I needed to secure an invitation to the Under Armour Senior Bowl all-star game. That would not only position me head-to-head against some of the best seniors in college football but also give me direct exposure to the coaching staffs of the two NFL teams that would coach in the game.

Adisa went to work on the Senior Bowl invite, and in mid-December I moved temporarily to Fort Lauderdale to improve my forty-yard dash time by working with Pete Bommarito of Perfect Competition Athletic Development. Pete was known as a speed guru who prepared pro prospects for the predraft NFL Combine.

This was back before college players started skipping bowl games to prepare for the draft. With no bowl game for Tulane, I had a head start working with Pete compared with other backs who still had a bowl game to play. That meant almost one-on-one speed coaching with Pete before the others began arriving.

On my first day with Pete, I ran a forty to establish a baseline. He timed me at 4.59. Terrible! I knew I was faster than that. Pete said I ran a slow time because I didn't know the proper way to run the forty.

"You have great natural top-end speed," Pete told me, meaning my maximum velocity was good enough for the NFL.

"We've got to work on your start," Pete continued. "The first ten yards are the most important. You cut down your time there and you will significantly reduce your forty time."

In other words, at my fastest, I was NFL-level fast. But I took too long while running the forty to reach my top speed.

So we went to work by evaluating film, and Pete taught me the science of running the forty. He pointed out mistakes in my technique. We focused on my start. Even though I placed the fingers of my right hand on the ground right up against the start line, my stance caused the rest of my body to be too far back. As a result, after making my first movement and starting to run, I still was at the start line. That meant the timer was going, yet most of my body was still at least forty yards from the finish line. Pete showed me how to leverage my flexibility to crowd the start line in my stance so that on my first movement I was stepping out past the start line. That way, I gained ground at the start instead of losing time.

Next, he showed me a trick for delaying by fractions of a second when the clock starter would start the timer. He said the starter would most likely be positioned to my right. In my start position, I had the fingers on my right hand on the ground and my left hand reaching behind me and visible above my back. My first motion in my start was to sweep my left arm forward. Because that movement was visible, it triggered the starter. Pete told me to lower that arm so my left hand was hidden behind my hip. My first movement with that hand would not be visible, and that would shave hundredths of a second off my time. And every hundredth of a second mattered.

Oddly, I would never use any of what Pete taught me on a football field. But even shaving a tenth of a second off my time in the forty could translate into being drafted several spots higher. Perhaps even a round earlier.

Pete also put me through strength training that made my legs more explosive. He taught me agility drills to improve my acceleration out of a move. Those were movements that I *could* take to the field.

While I was getting faster in Florida, Adisa was working the phones to land me a Senior Bowl invite, which proved surprisingly difficult.

You would think that a guy who ran for 2,100 yards would be a shoo-in for an all-star game. But apparently politics were involved in who received invites, and inviting the Tulane guy would not earn anyone any favors down the road. Still, Adisa stayed at it until an invite came at almost the last minute.

That led me to go into the game with a chip on my shoulder. So did what the draft pundits were saying about me. I wasn't listening to them, but my dad sure was. And he kept me informed about their knocks against me.

One was that Tulane didn't play in a competitive league. No, we didn't play in a major conference, but we played nonconference games against SEC schools. Were they watching when we played LSU my senior season and we ran the ball against the nation's best defense better than any other opponent to that point?

My dad told me one of the pundits said I didn't have "long speed." I didn't know what long speed was, or even if it was a measurable attribute. The best I could figure, long speed was the ability to avoid being caught from behind on long plays. I didn't know how I managed to score on as many long runs as I had without possessing "long speed."

It would have been easy to grow resentful at what I considered baseless criticisms. On the other hand, I didn't have to worry about getting a big head, thinking I was too good because the evaluators were making glowing comments about me. The antidote was to take such negative comments with a grain of salt. At the same time, I wanted to store them in the back of my mind to use as motivation.

The Senior Bowl was played on the last Saturday in January in Mobile, Alabama, on the off weekend between the NFL's conference championship games and Super Bowl XLII. The format was a North all-stars team vs. a South all-stars team. Each year, the coaching staffs from two NFL teams coached the Senior Bowl teams. That year, the San Francisco 49ers staff coached the South team, and the North was coached by the Oakland Raiders coaches.

The practices leading up to the game carried significance because they served as evaluation sessions, with coaches and scouts from every NFL team—except the Super Bowl team coaches—on hand. A lot of media members were there, too, not only to put their eyes on the crop of draft prospects but also because of the access to NFL and college coaches. The practices were set up for the players to showcase their skills. For me, that meant displaying my abilities as a ball carrier and also as a receiver and blocker in passing situations.

From a player's standpoint, Senior Bowl week provided me with the first taste of playing at the next level. During the daily practices, I had an opportunity to measure how I stacked up against the best draft prospects, including players with first-round grades. Just as when I attended the LSU and Auburn camps with the four- and five-star recruits in high school, there was not a moment during Senior Bowl practices when I felt I didn't belong on the field. The week also offered a sample of what it would be like to play for NFL coaches and have off-field meetings with them as part of their predraft evaluations.

I had solid practices throughout the week and went into the game confident that I was answering the questions about me. But I knew the game would be the ultimate proving ground.

I think I acquitted myself quite well—rushing for 59 yards on eight carries, and averaging more than seven yards per carry. I also caught a game-high four passes for 38 yards and made a tackle on special teams. My biggest play came with twenty-five seconds left in the game. We had a first down at the North's 15 yard line. I caught a screen pass from Tennessee quarterback Erik Ainge three yards behind the line of scrimmage, cut upfield, broke one tackle at the 11, broke a second tackle at the 6, and dragged a third defender to the 2. That set up a touchdown run by Florida receiver Andre Caldwell and an extra-point kick by Georgia's Brandon Coutu with no time on the clock, for a thrilling 17–16 win.

After the celebration, I was announced as the recipient of the game's Most Valuable Player award! I had proved I could play at that level of competition.

With the Senior Bowl box checked, I returned to Fort Lauderdale to prove to Pete that taking a week off from our performance training wouldn't hurt my forty time.

Showtime at the Combine

The annual NFL Combine is part skills display, part medical exam, part job interview, part cognitive testing, and part meat market. And, oh, yeah, part actual football on a field too!

All those elements make it an event for draft hopefuls that could determine which round they get drafted in or, in some cases, whether they play in the league at all. It's not an overstatement to say that football futures are at stake at the Combine. Even for players who are certain to be drafted, their performance at the Combine could move them up or down in the draft. Draft order translates directly into the amount of money they will receive in their rookie contract—sometimes a lot more or a lot less than they were expecting.

Each year, the NFL invites roughly three hundred of the top draft-eligible college players to Indianapolis' Lucas Oil Stadium, where they are evaluated in the same environment as the other prospects by scouts, coaches, and front-office decision-makers from every NFL team. In 2008, the Combine—officially, the National Invitational Camp—was held from Wednesday, February 20, through Tuesday, February 26, about two months before the draft.

Position groups were assigned specific days to attend, and running backs were grouped with quarterbacks and wide receivers. Sunday was our day for on-field workouts and drills, which received most of the public's attention because the NFL Network televised them. But that was only a portion of the evaluation process.

My time at the Combine felt weird because it was much more

in-depth than college recruiting. NFL teams' due diligence was understandable, considering they would invest hundreds of thousands to millions of dollars in the players they drafted. I didn't know if the Combine was intentionally set up to see if they could disrupt players' focus or see how we handled frustration, but the process was annoying at times.

Take the injury evaluation, for example. Every piece of a player's injury history was known, including minor injuries. Any part of his body that had been injured would get an X-ray and/or an MRI. Then if a right knee had been injured, for example, they would go ahead and get an MRI of the left knee as well. "You sprained an ankle before? Let's look at that, too." One MRI on my left knee took about forty-five minutes to an hour. Then they wanted to look at the other knee, which had not been injured. That was another forty-five to sixty minutes. I spent hours getting scanned and X-rayed.

They also tested me on a Biodex machine, which I had used while rehabbing from my knee surgery because it measured muscle strength for power and explosiveness. I had received a tip before the Combine that the Biodex test results would mean little in my overall evaluation, so I didn't need to risk straining a muscle before the on-field drills.

The off-field evaluation included taking the Wonderlic test to measure cognitive ability and problem-solving skills. The questions had nothing to do with football.

Every now and then, there's a media report about a player scoring extremely low on the Wonderlic. I have two thoughts, based on my experience. First, somebody from one of the teams likely leaked that player's score for it to be reported. Second, on my occasional glance around the room during the test, I saw looks of indifference on some of the guys' faces—which could be one reason they didn't score as well as they might have. The importance of a player's score probably relates directly to his position. I can see teams paying more attention to a quarterback's score because of the mental capacity needed to call two or three plays in the huddle and to quickly recognize defensive alignments and coverages.

Teams scheduled one-on-one interviews with prospects to get a feel for their personality and explore specific areas of interest. They used that time to watch film of the player in college or perhaps discuss their own team to see how the player processed their schemes and philosophy. They also worked in questions to test knowledge of the game, such as identifying defensive fronts and coverages.

The interviews could offer an idea of which teams were most interested in drafting a player. But not always. Sometimes teams don't show public interest in a player for draft-day strategic purposes. I talked briefly with Chicago Bears scout Chris Ballard at the Senior Bowl, but I had no other contact with anyone from the Bears—including at the Combine—until they drafted me.

Some players, especially those expected to be selected in the first round, might have to sit through fifteen to twenty team interviews. I interviewed with Pittsburgh, the Jets, and one other team I don't recall.

One of the teams asked about a game during my senior season when I wore a white sleeve on one leg but not the other. They probably were fishing for an unreported leg injury.

"I liked how the sleeve looked," I explained.

A few players skipped the Combine altogether. The ones from a large school with several draft prospects could have the scouts come to their campus and evaluate them there. That way, they could showcase their skills in a familiar, comfortable environment. Plus, forty times on a player's home campus seemed to be a little faster than at the Combine, where the timing system was more exact.

I determined before the Combine that I would do everything asked of me—every skill, drill, interview, medical exam, personality test, whatever. If I could go back to the Combine in a time machine, though, I would have said no to one thing.

Measuring height (I was 73.38 inches) and weight (217 pounds) took place on a stage. We were told to wear only tights. Then we walked across the stage so scouts could look us up and down to evaluate our body types. They looked us over so much that I felt like a piece of meat in a butcher shop. But, hey, I was a young dude aspiring to play in the NFL and willing to do anything to improve my draft stock. And I was not alone. Like sheep, the other players made the same walk across the stage. That's the part I could have done without. If I had it to do all over again, I would have said, "Y'all know my height and weight. There's no point in doing this."

No Regrets

The skills evaluations I remember included the bench press, vertical leap, broad jump, twenty-yard shuttle, and, of course, the forty-yard dash. On-field drills included running routes and catching balls. But the forty was the big one for me. To build my case for draft day positioning, the entire Combine experience came down to the forty.

This was the shot I wanted.

Players ran the forty twice at the Combine. Each player in a group ran his first forty before they started back with the first player, providing a bit of a break between the two runs.

In training sessions with Pete Bommarito, I had run a 4.3 a few times, so I was confident warming up at the Combine—though I definitely had a case of competitor's nerves before the first run. I had worked almost all my life to make it to the NFL, and I had prepared since mid-December for two runs that—hopefully—would take a combined nine seconds or less.

My first run felt good. As I walked back up the field to await my second run, I thought, *I think I'm fine. I'll be fine.* I felt the nerves lifting.

After completing my second run, I headed to pick up my bag. I took out my phone and saw text messages had already started coming in. On its broadcast, NFL Network said my unofficial time was 4.5. That was not the number I wanted. But my agent messaged me that the unofficial time on NFL Network was incorrect. He had my official times, and I ran a 4.44 both times.

What a relief after believing I had run a 4.5.

Adisa told me by text, "You did everything you needed to do to boost your draft stock so there are no questions about you."

The second box was now checked.

Chris Johnson, a running back from East Carolina, ran a 4.24 to break the Combine record. That dude was flying! They say records are made to be broken, but Chris's mark stood for *nine* years until Washington receiver John Ross clocked a 4.22. (Another seven years passed before Texas receiver Xavier Worthy lowered the record to 4.21.)

I shaved 0.15 seconds off my first timed run for Pete in Fort Lauderdale. Of the thirty running backs who ran the forty at the Combine, my time tied for eighth fastest. Later, when I could analyze the data, I discovered that I recorded one of the three fastest times over the first ten yards. I had to chuckle, remembering it was my starts that had hurt my forty times.

I left the Combine and returned home to Slidell free of regret.

Adisa was correct. I had put in the work I needed to. Under pressure, I performed to the level I needed. I answered the two main questions about me. I showed skeptics there was no reason to doubt me.

Now all I could do was wait for the draft. I had to be patient again, until I learned which team would make my NFL dream come true.

10

A NEW BEGINNING

"Who's going to draft you?"

"In which round will you go?"

"Where do you want to play?

Family and friends were enjoying the journey with me, and I was thrilled to share the draft anticipation with them. I don't know how many times I was asked those questions, but my answers were always the same.

"I don't know."

"I don't know."

"I don't care. I'll just be blessed to get drafted."

Getting drafted by New Orleans would have been cool, allowing me to play close to home and in Tulane's home stadium. But the Saints had Deuce McAllister at running back, and I didn't know how interested they would be in taking another running back in the first two rounds.

Though I had never lived anywhere but southern Louisiana, I

didn't consider weather a factor in choosing a team I wanted to play for. I was so excited about the draft process after checking those two boxes at the Senior Bowl and the Combine that I would have been happy to play for an NFL team in Timbuktu.

Regardless of which team drafted me, I would go all out to reward them for investing in me. I was about to become a professional athlete, and my job would be to be the best running back and teammate I could be. Maybe I could help turn around a franchise in the process. Anyone could play on a winning team, but helping change a franchise's dynamics and bringing consistency to its fans carried an intriguing appeal.

The running back class was strong and deep for the draft. Adisa was working his network and hearing that most teams ranked me as a second-round pick with the possibility of going late in the first round, depending on how many running backs were being selected and the needs of the teams at the bottom of the round. A few people were saying I could slide to the third round.

I visited the Saints facility because it was nearby and took a trip to Detroit to visit with the Lions. San Diego flew me in for a visit. At Tulane's Pro Day workouts, I met the Jacksonville Jaguars' running backs coach.

On the visits, I fielded the same questions I'd been asked at the Combine. I figured they already knew the types of answers I would give them but wanted to hear me articulate my answers and get a face-to-face feel for me as a person. Whatever questions they asked, I wanted my passion for football to show in my responses. I knew players for whom their honest answer for why they played football was because they were big or had the skill set to play the game. But passion for football carries a player through adversity, and I wanted to make it clear that I played because I loved the game.

The San Diego trip was interesting. Tim Hightower, another small-school running back, from Richmond, visited the Chargers facilities at the same time. On such visits, the expectation is to meet with the general manager, the head coach, and perhaps the offensive coordinator or running backs coach. I assumed because they paid to bring me in that they were serious about me and wanted their key decision-makers to spend time with me.

In San Diego, though, I didn't talk to the GM or the head coach. Two assistant coaches took Tim and me to dinner, and one was a defensive coach. Right from the start, the two coaches talked only to each other while Tim and I sat there trying to figure out what was going on. We both realized that the Chargers were not seriously considering drafting either one of us. Sometimes ahead of a draft, a team wants to appear to be looking in one direction when they are actually looking in another. If that was San Diego's strategy, having the media report about Tim and me meeting with the Chargers would serve as a smoke screen for the other teams trying to anticipate San Diego's draft day plans.

Tim and I decided to order the most expensive items on the menu because the bill wasn't coming out of our pockets. The visit allowed us to get to know each other pretty well by sharing our stories of the recruiting process. We had fun hanging out together. But I knew when I went home that I would not be telling people I thought the Chargers might draft me.

Waiting for the Call

The NFL draft consists of seven rounds, with the thirty-two teams selecting players in reverse order of their finish in the previous season. The team with the worst record drafts first, the team with the second-worst record chooses next, and that pattern continues through the reigning Super Bowl champion with the thirty-second pick. Then the order starts over for the second round.

Today, the draft is a three-day event, with only the first round on the first night for prime-time television. Rounds two and three are on day two, and the final four rounds are held on day three. In my draft year, 2008, the first two rounds were held on Saturday, April 26, with the third through seventh rounds on Sunday, April 27. I hoped I would learn my NFL destination on Saturday.

I intended to have a nice, small gathering at home with my family and a few friends to watch the draft unfold. I didn't want a draft party, in case my name wasn't called in the first two rounds. I would look silly throwing a big party for nothing.

I settled into our living room on Saturday afternoon to try to keep the day as relaxing as possible. Instead of anxiety or nervousness, I felt peace because I had done everything I needed to boost my draft stock as high as I believed it could go.

My parents, my brother, a few high school teammates, my college roommate Mike Parenton, and a few other Tulane teammates were with me. Then more people from Slidell started showing up. Family members from another state walked into the house. Then even more people started appearing. At one point, I looked out the window and saw more cars lining both sides of the street than you'll find on a used car lot.

I was wondering, *Why are these people here?*

The answer, in a word, was *Mom*. She wanted to have a party, so we did. She was having a blast cooking enough food in the kitchen to feed half of Slidell. As usual, Mom knew best because the flow of people into our party, with some keeping tabs from outside the house, created a gradual buildup.

The draft took place at Radio City Music Hall in New York City. There was no drama around the first pick, because Michigan offensive lineman Jake Long had agreed to a contract with the Miami Dolphins a few days before the draft, assuring his name would be the first one called by NFL commissioner Roger Goodell.

Teams were allotted ten minutes to make their first-round pick, and they usually took all their time, I guess in case some unexpected, can't-say-no trade offer came in last-minute from another team. With the number two pick, the St. Louis Rams selected Chris Long, a defensive end from Virginia. At number three, Atlanta picked Boston College quarterback Matt Ryan. Then, at the fourth spot, the draft got interesting, from my perspective, because the first running back was picked, with Arkansas' Darren McFadden going to the Oakland Raiders. That he would go first was no surprise, because Darren was highly rated coming out of an SEC school.

When the Saints' turn came with the seventh pick, I could feel the hopeful anticipation from our guests that the hometown team would choose me. But I didn't expect to hear my name yet. Actually, players waiting to be drafted in the first couple of rounds don't have to wait for their name to be called by the commissioner. Instead, they wait for their phone to ring with a call from the team on the clock, informing them they will be taking them with the next pick. No phone call came, and my name was not announced because the Saints went with defensive tackle Sedrick Ellis from USC.

The second running back off the board came at number thirteen, with Carolina nabbing Jonathan Stewart from Oregon. I expected Jonathan, coming out of a nationally recognized program, to be one of the first running backs chosen.

Then we went a while without hearing another running back's name, until Dallas chose Felix Jones out of Arkansas with the twenty-second pick. I was a little surprised by this pick because Felix had been Arkansas' number two back behind Darren McFadden, and he and I had run the same time (4.44) in the forty at the Combine.

Another running back went at number twenty-three, with Pittsburgh taking Illinois' Rashard Mendenhall. That pick intrigued me because even though Illinois played in the Big Ten Conference, it wasn't a powerhouse program. Still, Rashard had good size (five foot ten, 225 pounds) and speed (4.41), and his running style reminded me of former Heisman Trophy winner Ricky Williams.

Tennessee made it three running backs in a row, taking the record holder in the forty from the Combine, Chris Johnson from East Carolina, at number twenty-four. Chris also played in Conference USA, so the level of competition didn't prevent him from going in the first round. Teams cannot pass up 4.24 speed.

Considering his speed, I had expected Chris to go ahead of Felix. If he had, I probably would have started anticipating that my name would soon be called. Comparing myself to the backs who had been chosen, I didn't see any area (apart from Johnson's speed) where they stood out and I was deficient. I believed the biggest difference was the size of the programs they came from.

Now three-quarters of the way through the first round, I started paying more attention to which teams were on the clock and whether they had a need at my position. But the rest of the first round passed without another running back being selected.

The Bears

Early in the second round, three wide receivers were chosen, but no more running backs. As New Orleans' turn neared, our party perked up again. I had expected the Saints to go with a defensive player in the first round, and they had. But now I started to wonder whether they might want to acquire another running back after Deuce McAllister had missed most of the 2007 season because of a knee injury. However, with their pick at number forty, they went with Indiana defensive back Tracy Porter. Three picks later, after a couple of wide receivers came off the board, Minnesota drafted Tyrell Johnson, a defensive back from Arkansas State.

I had two cell phones—my personal phone and one Adisa had bought me for football business, with a number given only to NFL teams. As soon as the TV screen showed Chicago was on the clock for the next pick, my second phone rang.

Everyone in the house stopped their conversations and crowded into the living room so they could hear my end of the conversation.

It was Bears head coach Lovie Smith on the other end of the line.

"How you doing, big guy?" he asked. I would later learn that Lovie called everyone "big guy."

"I'm doing well," I replied. "How are you doing?"

"You ready to become a Chicago Bear?" Lovie asked.

"Yes, sir. Absolutely," I said, raising my other hand straight into the air. Our guests knew what that meant.

I don't remember what Lovie said the rest of the conversation, but when I clicked off the call, everyone erupted in celebration. I hugged my parents. My brother and teammates who were closest to me squeezed in to embrace and high-five me. Within seconds, everybody inside our house was trying to grab a piece of me to hug.

As soon as the celebration settled, Mom and Dad called me back to my bedroom for a quiet moment together. Dad was the last one into the room and closed the door behind him.

"We're going to pray for you now," he said.

He prayed for health and success, and for the opportunity I had been given to glorify God through the way I play football.

My parents knew exactly what I needed. Amid all the screaming and hollering because I had been drafted, I needed to be reoriented, to not get too high on myself. That prayer refocused me on the purpose I had pursued from the moment I learned to carry a football. The time alone with my parents also reemphasized the importance of prayer.

Before we rejoined the party, Dad said to Mom, "Our son has just been drafted by the Bears in the second round!"

She smiled as she looked into my eyes.

"We're proud of you," Dad told me. "But you know this is just the beginning, right?"

The tone in his voice was the same as the day when he'd told me, "That's football, Son."

This is just the beginning.

I immediately began processing Dad's words.

He's right. I haven't done a thing in the NFL yet, and I'm getting all these congratulations. I still have a long road ahead of me to represent my family, and to represent the Bears in the right way.

It was a special moment amid an exciting celebration with my family and friends. My dream was coming true. And I was ready to go play in the NFL with passion and with purpose. But this was only the beginning.

First Impressions

Having grown up in southern Louisiana, I knew very little about the Bears. On top of that, I was born in 1985, so the great Bears team that made the Super Bowl Shuffle famous, that defeated New England in Super Bowl XX, that had Walter Payton and Mike Singletary and Richard Dent and William "Refrigerator" Perry—that was all before my time.

I didn't know the Bears' history—that George Halas, one of the NFL's founders, started a team called the Decatur Staleys in 1920, moved them to Chicago in 1921, and renamed his team the Chicago Bears. The new team played their first season at Cubs Park, which later became known as Wrigley Field and is still the home of the Cubs baseball team. And I didn't know that at the time I was drafted, the Bears had the most players in the Pro Football Hall of Fame and had retired more numbers of former players than any NFL team.

If it helps, Bears fans, I did root for the Bears against Indianapolis in Super Bowl XLI because I had studied Devin Hester as a kick returner that season, his rookie year. When he returned the opening kickoff for a touchdown, I thought there was no way Chicago would lose that game. But Peyton Manning brought the Colts from behind to win the championship.

My roommate, Mike, knew football history better than I did, and he bought me a Bears history book and the movie *Brian's Song*, which we watched together.

Brian's Song is a made-for-TV movie from the 1970s about two Bears players, Gale Sayers, who was Black, and Brian Piccolo, who was white. Both were running backs, and they were the first interracial roommates in NFL history. The movie showed how they put their racial differences aside to become close friends, and how that affected both men when Piccolo became sick with cancer and eventually died.

I loved the movie and gained a ton of respect for what football players in that era endured to stay in the sport, the talent Gale Sayers displayed before injuries forced him to retire early, and the impact Brian Piccolo had on those around him because of how he lived his life.

Brian's Song is considered one of the all-time great guy-cry movies—though, for the record, I didn't shed any tears. As much as my wife would like me to become one, I'm not a crier. When the movie concluded, Mike, who is white, said, "That's kind of like you and me. But, hopefully, I don't die."

After Brian Piccolo died in 1970, the Bears created the Brian Piccolo Award, which has been awarded annually ever since to one rookie and one veteran who best exemplify Piccolo's "courage, loyalty, teamwork, dedication, and sense of humor."

Saying Thank You

Through the collective bargaining agreement (CBA) with the NFL Players Association, the team owners established a system for rookie contracts that works in their favor. The length of contracts for drafted players is predetermined based on the round selected, and salaries are slotted by draft position. In other words, the player selected just ahead of me in the draft would be paid more than I was, and I would make more than the players chosen after me. That is one reason draft prospects want to improve their stock to be selected as high in the draft as possible.

My rookie contract was for four years and roughly $3.8 million, including a $1.5 million signing bonus. According to the CBA rules, my salary was not guaranteed. I would receive the full salary only if I fulfilled all four years of the contract. If the team cut me after my first season, I would not be paid for the remaining three years, though I would keep the signing bonus.

Too many NFL rookies learn an important lesson the hard way: Don't spend what you haven't earned yet.

With my signing bonus, I wanted to do something nice for my parents. Their house was paid for, so I decided to buy each something they were unlikely to purchase for themselves. I bought my dad a Rolex. He wasn't necessarily a watch guy, but he did appreciate a nice timepiece. I bought my mom a diamond bracelet. She hadn't worked when Bryan and I were growing up so she could be home with us. But after we were out of the house, Mom took a job in the jewelry department at JCPenney. Even today when she dresses up for special occasions, she wears that bracelet.

Mom and Dad had sacrificed so much to support Bryan and me in all of our sports. They made it look easy getting us to practice, games, and tournaments year-round. When we were older and had games that overlapped, they split up so that one of them would be at each one of our games. And then they would switch the next time there was an overlap. During one basketball season, my mom drove a one-hour round trip to take me to practice. I could never repay my parents for all they sacrificed and provided, but it felt good to at least give them gifts to express my appreciation.

Getting Down to Business

My first trip to Chicago—ever—came a week after the draft, when I reported to the Bears' rookie minicamp.

The camp consisted of thirty to forty players with a mix of new draft picks and undrafted free agents. The free agents were either given a shot at making the team or signed to have enough bodies to field an offense and a defense during camp.

For my first day on the job, I wanted to look the part of a professional. I owned two or three suits, so I picked out my best suit and tie to wear when I reported for work at the Bears' headquarters, Halas Hall, in suburban Lake Forest, Illinois.

When I walked into the team meeting room, I looked around and noticed the other players were wearing sweatpants or shorts and T-shirts. Their facial expressions were a mixture of, "Did I miss the memo?" and "Who does this guy think he is?"

First impressions are important, and I was a professional now. It was cool to have been drafted, and I was living a dream by playing in the NFL; but I wanted to show that I meant business. It only seemed right to dress professionally for my first time inside Halas Hall.

When Lovie Smith entered the room, he noticed my suit right away. How could he not? While addressing the rookies, he pointed toward me.

"This is serious business," he said. "He took it upon himself to wear a suit his first day. That's how you should think about who you are, what you're going into, and how you'll present yourself."

When the equipment staff handed out gear, the number I had worn since high school and through Tulane, number 25, already belonged to another running back, Garrett Wolfe. I had also worn 25 my first year in youth football, before switching the next year to 22. My dad was a Texan, and the Cowboys' Emmitt Smith, one of my favorite running backs, wore 22 for Dallas. When I learned I couldn't have 25 with the Bears but that 22 was available, I happily said, "I'll take that."

11

WELCOME TO THE NFL

Unlike my first season at Tulane, I didn't start out at the bottom of the depth chart with the Bears. When I was drafted, Cedric Benson was the Bears' starting running back. He had been the fourth overall pick in the 2005 draft and was entering his fourth year in the league, so the Bears had invested some time and money in him. But then the team waived him because of off-field issues.

When training camp opened, I was one of five backs in full competition for the starting job, along with veteran Adrian Peterson (not the same Adrian Peterson my agent had compared me to), Garrett Wolfe, P. J. Pope, and rookie Matt Lawrence. There was also a possibility the team would bring in another potential starter through free agency or a trade before the season started.

Just like when I was seven, I had a first-practice moment at age twenty-two that opened my eyes to the reality of what I had just stepped into.

This one occurred on our first day in full pads.

We were in a nine-on-seven drill designed to help the defense against the run game. The offense had nine players, with no wide receivers, and the defense had its front seven for stopping the run. Basically, the seven defenders went up against seven blockers, because the quarterback wasn't blocking and I would be the ball carrier. If one defender could get past his blocker, odds were that he and I would have an impromptu meeting in the backfield. Nine-on-seven is an old-school football drill.

I was looking at the defense and seeing the likes of Brian Urlacher, Lance Briggs, Tommie Harris, Charles "Peanut" Tillman, Adewale Ogunleye, and Alex Brown—all experienced starters who had played in the Super Bowl two seasons earlier.

The play was 16 Power O, a handoff to me going right. At the snap, the left or backside guard would pull toward the right side of the line. The play required the pulling guard to have vision like a running back to know who to block. The rest of the offensive line would block at angles to their left, and the fullback would be the lead blocker and kick out the defensive end to the offense's right. If the backside guard saw a hole open in the line's blocking, he would turn through that opening and block the linebacker to prevent him from penetrating the line and blowing up the play in the backfield. If the O-linemen were on their blocks, he would continue around to the hole inside where the fullback was kicking out the end and block the linebacker there. Then I would run through that massive opening and go score a touchdown!

Kyle Orton was at quarterback, and as he stood behind center looking over the defensive alignment and made his pre-snap calls, Urlacher—the veteran middle linebacker—called out "Strong left! Strong left!" based on the offensive alignment.

As Kyle went under center and barked out, “Red 18! Red 18!” as part of his snap cadence, the tight end went in motion. Urlacher immediately shouted, “It’s coming here! It’s coming A gap!”

The center snapped the ball, and Kyle handed it off to me. I saw a gap open right before the pulling guard cut in to make his block on the linebacker. But because Urlacher had called out the play, the backside linebacker, Lance Briggs, knew that he needed to crash over the top of the blocking scheme, step into the forming hole, and take on the pulling guard. That freed up Urlacher from being blocked by the guard, allowing him to fill what was once a promising hole and make the tackle. We were in training camp, so Urlacher only bumped me instead of tackling me, but the play was dead from the beginning because the veteran players on defense had recognized it before the snap. They had probably seen it run live and on film hundreds of times.

I returned to the huddle asking myself how we were ever going to run a successful play if the defense always knew where the play was going.

I also knew that, in a game, the middle linebacker would not just give me a friendly bump.

Welcome to the NFL, rookie!

Making the Jump

I learned how to be an NFL player by watching teammates like Brian Urlacher, Peanut Tillman, and Lance Briggs. Brian is in the Hall of Fame, and I believe Peanut and Lance should be. They modeled for me how to prepare myself in every aspect of the game. They worked hard in the weight room, stayed after practice for extra reps, and spent time with their position coaches breaking down film—not just of opponents but also of themselves—to identify areas to improve.

Mike Brown, the quintessential veteran safety in the NFL, made me a better back in the open field by emphasizing the need to be decisive when making a move and teaching me to understand leverage so I would keep my pads down even when running at full speed.

My aim wasn't only to win the starting job. I wanted to be involved in every facet of the offense, to play every down. I wanted to stay on the field. That meant working to improve my ability to pick up blocks on the bigger defensive linemen and linebackers who penetrated our backfield on a hunt for our quarterback.

Learning the offensive playbook presented the first challenge, because if you don't know what to do on a play, the coaches won't put you out there.

The playbook was a binder probably eight inches thick and filled with everything from formations to how to run the same plays five, six, seven different ways. It covered our plan for facing specific defenses. I had to learn the plays and formations and also how to process them quickly—because, for the first time in my career, I was hearing two and sometimes three plays called in the huddle. Having multiple plays called allows the quarterback to check at the line of scrimmage to the best one, depending on what he sees from the defense.

I had started working on memorizing the playbook during the rookie minicamp. At night at the hotel, I stayed in my room to study. The coaches had a plan for installing the playbook in sections. I read ahead to prepare for the next installation period.

What people say about the speed of the game being so much faster in the NFL is true. I learned that this high level of speed came from players knowing exactly what to do, which allowed them to anticipate sooner and react faster.

The communication at the line of scrimmage was also more complex in the pros than in college. On offense, the center called protections for the rest of the O-line. The quarterback made his calls, including sometimes switching to another play called in the huddle. Defenders made the same types of calls on their side of the line and threw in the occasional trash talk to the offense. I had to learn to focus on my job for each play, and then when the ball was snapped, rely on talent and instinct. When a play broke down, the ability to still make something positive happen separated the special player from the average player who might possess elite talent but could only do what the play call told him to do. Rookies especially could look robotic out there because they struggled to adapt in the middle of a play.

The ability to adapt on the fly required me not only to learn my own job on a play but also to understand the *purpose* of the play. For example, on a pass play, let's say I was supposed to leave the backfield as a checkdown option for the quarterback if the downfield receivers weren't open or a blitz forced him to release the ball early. If I recognized that the defense was playing zone and saw a defender sitting on the outside of the play, I knew that a primary receiver would be crossing into the zone where that defender would be sitting, and I would have to adjust my route to bring the defender toward me and help the crossing receiver get open.

The key was to learn the plays so well that, when I heard the play call in the huddle, I didn't need to ask myself, *Okay, what do I do on this play?* Because if I were in the backfield thinking about what I was supposed to do at the snap, I would not see before the snap what the defense was doing. That's where a rookie could really get into trouble, because not seeing the big picture prevented him from playing fast in a league where everyone around him was at top speed.

Playing fast started with learning the playbook.

Another challenge was how practices were set up to prevent injuries. The organized team activities (OTAs) before training camp were noncontact practices. OTAs were a critical time for me to apply on the field what I was learning through studying the playbook and film. We didn't wear full pads during OTAs, just soft-shell helmets to protect our heads. Without pads, blocking at the line of scrimmage was more about assignments and techniques than simulating game action. Holes in the NFL are sometimes more accurately described as creases because of how small they can be. Whatever you prefer to call them, they also don't stay open very long. I had to hit the holes at just the right time, or a play would probably not succeed. But it wasn't until training camp that I could experience gamelike speed to prepare for my first regular season.

Tim Spencer was the Bears' running backs coach for my first five seasons. He was as impactful for me in the NFL as Greg Davis Jr. had been at Tulane. Tim held his backs to a high standard, and he even had a fine system that made us pay $25 to $50 for every ball we dropped during practice. A missed assignment cost $500. A fumble set us back $1,000. The fines went into a team pot to buy Christmas gifts, but nobody wanted to contribute to that good cause. The root of mistakes during games usually was mistakes during practices, and Tim made sure we didn't get sloppy in practice.

As camp progressed, the competition for the starting spot seemed to be coming down to Garrett Wolfe and me. But then Garrett injured his hamstring. Kevin Jones, a free agent and former Detroit starter, had signed a one-year contract with us in July. He was coming back from a knee injury, and with Garrett's hamstring problem, speculation shifted to a potential one-two punch of me and Kevin sharing carries.

After our fourth and final preseason game, when the final fifty-three-man roster was being set, Lovie called me into his office. I don't remember whether he and I had interacted with each other during camp, because Lovie spent his time with the defense.

"I've stayed away from you so you could focus on the playbook," Lovie told me. "I didn't want to be telling you a bunch of stuff because I didn't want us to over-coach you. I just wanted to see how you would handle your reps and having to learn the playbook and do all the other stuff you had to do. You handled all that well, and you're going to be the starter in week one."

THE EARLY YEARS

Me celebrating the Bears' 1986 Super Bowl victory.

My second year playing in the Slidell Youth Football Association, I wore the number that would define my entire career.

My brother, Bryan (*right*), and me with our dad, "Coach Gene," in 1994. Check out the eight-inch battle scar on Dad's left knee. Dude had a matching set. But like he said, "That's football, Son."

By my sophomore year at Slidell High School, I had lost my lucky number but gained a little more height, speed, and strength.

My senior year, I rushed for more than 200 yards five times.

It wasn't until I gained 342 yards on 38 carries and scored four touchdowns against SMU that agents finally started to take notice of that guy from Tulane.

On April 26, 2008, I got the phone call that changed my life. With the 44th pick of the draft, I officially became a Chicago Bear.

After declining a lowball extension offer, I opened the 2011 season with 158 total yards and a TD, kicking off the "Pay Forté" movement in Chicago. And I made the Pro Bowl.

I didn't often go airborne, but when we got down to the goal line against the Seahawks in the 2011 Divisional Playoffs, I went all out. I came up a little short, but we still won the game 35–24.

After a great 2011 season, Peanut Tillman (*left*), Corey Graham (*right*), and I were chosen to represent the Bears at the 2012 Pro Bowl in Honolulu, Hawaii. It was a tough gig, but someone had to do it.

Postgame victory shot in 2012. *Front row, left to right:* Alshon Jeffery, Devin Hester, Tim Jennings, Brandon Marshall. *Middle row:* Joe Anderson, Major Wright (21), Eric Weems, Kelvin Hayden, me. (Sorry I'm so blurry, I'm just that fast.) *Back row:* J. T. Thomas (97), Anthony Walters (37), Amobi Okoye, Corey Wootton.

TO GOD BE THE GLORY.

Danielle could not stop smiling after she saw how neat and tidy my locker was.

What can I say?
We clean up well.

Huddling up at a Find Your Forté mentoring session.

Team Forté (*left to right*): Jaden, Danielle, Nia, me, Matthew, Nahla.

EVERY. DOWN. BACK.

I nodded and thanked him. I didn't smile until I was walking out the door and knew he couldn't see my face.

I was excited to have earned the starting position, but thinking back to the conversation with my parents on draft day, I hadn't done anything yet. I was still just beginning.

"Something Special?"

I didn't pay much attention to the media during my NFL career. My dad had kept me updated on what the draft pundits said about me at Tulane. Now that I was playing in a major media market, I didn't have to seek out information because it usually found its way to me anyway.

Case in point: After the media learned that I was the starting running back, a group of reporters gathered around me for an interview. One asked if I knew I would be the Bears' first rookie to start at my position since Walter Payton in 1975. I didn't. Payton was the greatest running back of all time, and it was an honor to have my name mentioned in the same sentence as his—even if that sentence was, "Matt Forté is no Walter Payton."

Then the reporter asked if I knew Payton's stats in his first NFL game. Though I had been learning Bears history, I didn't know the answer. The reporter told me that Payton, in his first game, had eight carries for zero yards against the Baltimore Colts.

"I'm hoping to do better than that," I replied, and the reporters laughed.

Our first game of the season was also against the Colts—now located in Indianapolis—on *Sunday Night Football.* You couldn't ask for anything better: a prime-time TV slot with a national viewing audience; Louisiana native Peyton Manning quarterbacking the Colts in a rematch of the 2007 Super Bowl; and the first regular-season game in the Colts' new Lucas Oil Stadium. The only way I might have rewritten the script would've been to make it a home game at Soldier Field. But at least I was returning to the site of the NFL Combine, where I had cemented my place in the draft. Why not turn in another clutch performance in Indy?

I had watched the Bears–Colts Super Bowl when I was still a college kid in Louisiana. Now, more than thirty of my new teammates were guys who had been in that game. The anticipation in our locker room, and among our fans in Chicago, made the first game of the season feel almost like playing in a Super Bowl to start my career.

In the week leading up to the game, friends and family asked me if I was nervous.

Uh, yeah! Some players lie and say they are calm before a big game. I felt anxiety and pressure before *every* game—all the way through my tenth season in the league. Before each game, the butterflies fluttered in my stomach until the first play when I was on the field. If we kicked off to start the game, the butterflies remained while our defense was on the field. I had to be involved in a play to make them leave. Even if I didn't touch the ball on our first offensive snap, I looked for someone to hit on the defense. Only then could I say, "All right, *now* we're playing football" and chase the butterflies away.

Running back is a pressure-packed position, because the ball carrier holds the fate of his team in his hands. No back ever wants to drop the ball. Especially in front of a national, Sunday-night audience that we knew included our rivals from around the league, who were home after playing their own games earlier in the day.

Playing my first game with a new team at a new level of football meant developing new routines. Or finding ways to bring my previous routines with me.

One of my routines was attending the pregame chapel for players and coaches.

At Tulane, I had attended church on Sundays and Fellowship of Christian Athletes meetings during the week. I was committed to being a Christian, but I had not yet moved beyond my shallow thinking that doing things in the name of religion—such as attending church and FCA—would lead to good things happening on the football field. Entering the NFL, there was no question that I would attend pregame chapels. Going was an automatic for me. I also faithfully attended weekly Bible studies during the season. As a kid, I knew that whenever the church doors were open, the Fortés would be there. And I carried those religious routines with me to the NFL.

At the chapel meeting before my first game, the chaplain started talking about God's grace.

"God is not our genie," he said. "He's not a good luck charm for you to use only when you need Him."

Wham! That statement immediately convicted me. I had to admit that was how I had been living my life.

The message centered on how we are saved by grace through faith. We didn't earn our salvation, the chaplain said. We could never do enough to earn our salvation, and we could never do enough to lose it, either—because, when Jesus died on the cross for our sins, He did all the work necessary. Because of what Jesus has done for us, we should be gracious and always seek after Him and love Him.

I could imagine God saying to me, "Matt, you've been using me like a good luck charm, but I'm still so gracious that I am going to allow you to understand that my ways are higher than yours. My thoughts are higher than yours."[1]

After the chapel ended, the chaplain came up to me.

"You excited about tonight?" he asked.

"Yeah, I'm excited," I said.

"Man," he told me, "I just feel like there's something special that's going to happen."

That was all he said before he walked away, leaving me to wonder what he meant.

---

[1] See Isaiah 55:8-9.

Touchdown!

Before pregame warm-ups, I went through another one of my regular routines: dressing for the game. First, I looked at my uniform in my locker. The white pants with an orange stripe trimmed in navy blue down the outside of each leg. The long white socks with the navy-orange-navy stripes above the calves. The white jersey with the same navy-orange-navy stripe pattern on the sleeves, and the number 22 in navy with orange trim on the front. On the back, I proudly read the name FORTE stitched across the shoulders and thought of everything that name stood for. And then the navy blue helmet with the iconic wishbone-C logo in orange with white trim on each side.

As I would before every game over the next ten years, I dressed in this order: pants, socks, undershirt, and jersey (over my shoulder pads). Then I had both wrists taped, and I returned to my locker to put on my gloves. Lastly, I laced up my cleats and headed out to the field for pregame warm-ups.

My parents had flown to Indianapolis for my NFL debut. I knew the location of their tickets, and during warm-ups I looked way up into the nosebleed seats in one of the corner sections. I was accustomed to large indoor stadiums from playing in the Superdome, but their seats were so far from the field that I couldn't be certain I was looking in the right place. At one point, I thought I recognized them, and I waved; but I couldn't tell if they saw me waving.

We kicked off to start the game, so I had to endure my pregame butterflies a little longer. Our defense put the Colts in a third-and-six on their first possession, but Peyton Manning completed a pass for a first down—extending the life of my butterflies. Our defense forced the Colts to punt without gaining another first down. Devin Hester fielded the punt inside our 10 yard line and made an exciting return beyond the 30. (All of Devin's punt returns were exciting!)

Finally, I could take the field and get that first hit in.

On our first play, the exchange between the center and the quarterback went wonky, and the ball hit the turf and squirted free toward me. I lunged forward to try to recover it, and two Colts defenders dove across my back. That was not the first contact I wanted! Fortunately, the referees had whistled the play dead because of a false start penalty for an illegal snap. You can go months without seeing a false start on the center—I mean, the play doesn't *start* until he snaps the ball. But we got one on our first play of the season.

Our first official play was a handoff to me. I got stacked up at the line of scrimmage for a one-yard gain. The coaches called my number again on the next play, and I found a crease for a six-yard gain up the middle. After an incomplete pass on third down, we punted. So, while it wasn't the sustained drive I was hoping for, it was nice to have that first possession under my belt.

Manning and the Colts offense put together a nice drive on their next possession, but our defense held them to a field goal and a 3–0 Indy lead.

We started our next possession at our own 46. I ran for four yards on the first play, and Kyle threw an incomplete pass on second down, setting up a third-and-six at the midfield stripe.

Our scouting report said that Indianapolis tended to play Tampa-2 coverage in third-down situations and split their defensive line in a 2-3—meaning their two defensive ends would line up wide of our offensive tackles, with their two interior linemen in the gaps between our guards and tackles (three-technique, if you're familiar with football terminology). The middle linebacker, who had pass-defense responsibilities, would stand about eight yards off the ball, leaving their defense vulnerable to a run up the middle.

If we got that look from Indy, we knew they would be expecting a pass, and we wanted to run a trap play. As we broke the huddle, I saw that the defense was aligned precisely as we'd hoped.

At the snap, I took a drop step to allow our left guard, Josh

Beekman, time to pull to the right. Right guard Roberto Garza ignored the defensive tackle lined up to his right and stepped forward into the second level to block the middle linebacker (known as the Mike). As the play-side defensive tackle charged into the backfield, Josh executed a great trap block to take him out of the play. With everyone else on their blocks, all I needed in order to gain the first down was for Roberto to take out the Mike. He did, hitting him thigh high to take his legs out from under him. As I broke into the open field, I saw the free safety coming in at an angle from my right. I juked him with a quick move, and then all I needed to do was outrun the strong safety—which I did, displaying my, ahem, long speed to take the ball to the house for a fifty-yard touchdown.

Over the final thirty yards, when it was a footrace with the safety, I felt an amazing sensation of a wind behind me, pushing me forward at a higher speed than normal.

As I crossed the goal line, I let out a loud, "Ahhhhhhhhhh!" like I was in disbelief of what had just happened. I didn't know what else to say! As the course of my NFL career would prove, it was difficult enough getting to the second and third levels of the defense in the NFL, let alone breaking a long run against a defense as stout and well-coached as Indy's.

I hadn't planned a touchdown celebration, so I improvised one on the spot. As I stopped at the back of the end zone, I switched the ball from my right hand to my left and pointed my right index finger heavenward to thank God for allowing me the opportunity to play in the NFL. All glory belonged to Him!

For His Glory

One other memorable moment stands out from my first game.

I've shared my welcome-to-the-NFL moment when Brian Urlacher called out our play in practice before we snapped the ball. That was my experiential welcome to the league. My physical welcome came in the second quarter of the Colts game.

A screen pass is one of the scariest plays for a running back, because you catch the ball with your back to the defense and have no idea where the defenders are while the pass floats in the air for an hour (or so it seems). That's usually why, when a running back drops a screen pass, you'll see on the slow-motion replay that he turned his head too soon to look upfield, taking his eye off the ball before it reached his hands.

We ran a screen to the left, and I caught the pass and turned upfield to tuck in behind my blockers. Linebacker Clint Session came through a gap and tried to make the tackle. As we collided, he dropped down and grabbed my right ankle. I stayed on my feet and tried to step out of the tackle to gain more yardage.

This is awesome! I thought. *I'm dragging a big guy and getting extra yards!*

I was a rookie with a lot to learn.

As I surged forward, I stood too tall, making myself an easy target for the hard-hitting Bob Sanders, who came flying in from his safety spot. Coach Davis at Tulane had taught me that the great running backs evade square hits, but I saw Bob too late to make a move. He hit me square on my left shoulder, including underneath the shoulder pad where it hangs over the arm. He hit me so hard that he stopped my forward momentum and spun me to the right as I fell to the ground. It was one of those hits where I could hear the crowd release a collective "Oooohhh."

I tried to get up, but my left arm was dead. I couldn't move it. Two teammates helped me to my feet, and I jogged to the sideline, dragging my left arm with me. Bobby Slater, one of my favorite Bears trainers, came to check on me.

"Got you good with that one, huh?" he said.

Bobby grabbed a container of Tiger Balm or Icy Hot and rubbed it into my shoulder.

"That should loosen it up," he told me. "Let me know if the feeling doesn't come back."

He grabbed my left hand and told me to squeeze. In about fifteen seconds, the feeling started coming back to my hand. The strength returned to my squeeze.

"You good to go?" Bobby asked.

"Yep," I said, and went back into the game.

Rookie lesson learned: Sometimes it's better just to go down rather than expose yourself to a big hit by fighting for another yard or two you're probably not going to get. You can try to gain that yard or two on the next play—unless you're standing on the sideline with a trainer.

We defeated the Colts 29–13, and I finished the game with 123 yards on twenty-three carries and that long touchdown run. I broke the franchise record for rushing yards in a first game.

My big debut earned me the *Sunday Night Football* broadcast's Horse Trailer Player of the Game award. NBC sideline reporter Andrea Kremer interviewed me on camera after the game. When she asked her first question, the pregame chapel service and the brief conversation with the chaplain came to mind.

This is what he was talking about, I realized.

I used the interview to share my faith with the TV audience. I said I couldn't take credit for myself and needed to give all credit to Jesus Christ. He had given me the talent to make it to the NFL, and He deserved all the glory. After using Him for my own benefit for too long, I wanted Him to be glorified through my running the football.

Record-Setting Rookie

We finished the season at 9–7, one game behind division-leader Minnesota in the NFC North. I turned in three 100-yard rushing games en route to a season total of 1,238 yards and eight touchdowns on 316 carries. The rushing yards and number of carries were the most ever by a Bears rookie. As an every-down back, I also caught a franchise-record sixty-three passes for 477 yards and four scores. My 1,715 yards from scrimmage were third in the league and broke the Bears record set by Gale Sayers in 1965.

Not only did I now have my name associated with Sayers, but I also received the rookie portion of the Brian Piccolo Award. (I also later won the award as a veteran.) Having that honor given to me by the team meant a lot, because it represented more than football skills; it represented the characteristics of a good person. I knew those characteristics resulted from the values my parents had instilled in me growing up. The award was as much theirs as mine.

I had not forgotten the story of Sayers and Piccolo after Mike Parenton introduced it to me. I had also gained knowledge of the franchise's deep history. I would never try to give myself the status of a Bears legend such as Walter Payton, Gale Sayers, or Brian Piccolo. But having my name mentioned alongside theirs gave me an appreciation for how special it was to play for the Bears.

Once again, God, in His providence, graciously gave me more than I deserved. I should have been doing more for Him than simply talking about Him in a postgame interview or pointing toward heaven when I scored a touchdown. It should have been my *life* that was pointing people toward God. And it wasn't.

12

THROWN FOR A LOSS

After my rookie season, I had an opportunity to make a paid appearance at a national magazine's Super Bowl party in Tampa, Florida. While I was there, I met a young woman named Danielle, who was working for a public relations and marketing firm in Chicago while also a full-time college student. One of my teammates was a client of Danielle's boss, and apparently he and the boss had been trying to play matchmaker for Danielle and me. We finally met at Super Bowl XLIII.

Danielle's father is a pastor, and when Danielle met me, I was holding a drink. She asked what I was drinking.

"Cranberry juice," I said.

She smelled the drink to make sure I was telling the truth.

"I don't drink alcohol," I told her.

After I passed that test, we started a conversation. Our faith stories came up early, and I liked how genuine she was. We wound up having a good discussion—until my agent interrupted to remind me that I was getting paid to be at the party and suggested I should mingle more to avoid being accused of breach of contract.

That was the offseason when I had planned to finish my degree at Tulane; but I told Danielle that when I returned to Chicago, I would like somebody to show me around the city.

While I was in Louisiana, we talked often on Skype and began to forge a relationship. I asked her a few times to write a paper for me, but she declined each time. She did, however, look over my papers after I had written them and make suggestions that improved them.

Finishing What I Had Started

When I had decided to delay my graduation from Tulane to prepare for the NFL draft, I promised myself I would finish my degree during my first offseason. I knew the longer I waited to go back to school, the less likely I would be to follow through.

Having completed all but my final semester, I needed only twelve hours—four classes—to earn my bachelor's degree in finance. But after a full year away from school, my commitment was tested. I found it challenging to get my head back in the game academically, and I battled days of not wanting to go to class.

Returning to school was important to me, however, because I wanted to finish what I had started. I had done the work to get through seven semesters as a student-athlete, and I would not allow myself to stop short of the finish line. My dad had graduated from Tulane, and I wanted to share the status of Tulane graduate with him. I also believed I owed it to the university because of the honor they had given me by awarding me a football scholarship. That scholarship ended when I left school, and it didn't cover my final semester; but the NFL's tuition reimbursement program for players kept me from having to dip into my signing bonus.

This time around, I was much better known on campus and garnered a lot more attention. I could guess which students followed football because they whispered to each other the first time I walked into a classroom. Apparently they thought I couldn't tell they were talking about me.

My communications professor was very sweet—and definitely not a football fan. One day during class, she said, "I hear we have someone special in our class. Mr. Forté, they say you're an athlete. Do you play for Tulane?"

The football fans in the class laughed.

"No, ma'am," I replied. "I used to play for Tulane, but I don't anymore."

"Oh," she said. "Who do you play for?"

"The Chicago Bears."

"Oh, really?" she responded. "Chicago? Is that in the NFL?"

"Yes, ma'am."

The funniest part was watching the other guys in the room biting their lips, trying not to laugh too hard.

While I played football at Tulane, I took my classes seriously. Tulane is a strong academic school, and I was not one of those college athletes whose academic goal was simply to remain eligible for sports. My parents had drilled into Bryan and me the importance of an education, and earning my degree remains one of my most treasured accomplishments.

With part of my signing bonus, I had bought a BMW 6 Series convertible that I drove around campus, top down, because I wanted to look cool. I wanted people to see me driving my car and think, *Hey, that's Matt!* I could be friends with anyone I wanted. I could gain access to practically any place I wanted to go on campus. I thought I was the coolest guy on the planet.

Not the Same

While I was at Tulane, learning to build PowerPoint presentations and deliver speeches without reading from note cards, the Bears acquired quarterback Jay Cutler in a trade with the Denver Broncos. Jay's arrival upped the expectations for our team going into the 2009 season. There were many who saw him as the missing piece our team needed to get to the next level.

In June OTAs, I caught a five-yard pass on a simple checkdown. When I turned upfield and started running, my left hamstring popped and I crumpled to the ground. The Chicago media didn't cover OTAs as heavily as they did the regular season, so there weren't many reporters around. That made it easier for the team to keep the injury relatively quiet. From what I heard, the media reports were that my injury was not that big of a deal.

Those reports were wrong. I knew it was bad.

I called my dad the day it happened.

"How you doing?" he asked.

"We had practice today," I said, delaying the reason for the call. "I tore my hamstring."

I heard him take a deep breath.

The hamstring had torn behind the knee. After consulting with the team doctors, I opted not to have surgery, in favor of allowing the hamstring to heal with rest.

Later I would look back at my injury as a time when God was trying to get my attention; but in the midst of the experience, I didn't hear the alarm bells that were going off in my life.

I was still doing good things on the outside but had not yet experienced transformation on the inside. I attended church during the offseason and looked forward to participating in chapel services and Bible studies during the year. I had publicly shared my faith after the *Sunday Night Football* game, and I had a routine for celebrating touchdowns that included pointing toward heaven to give the glory to God.

For a long time, God had been placing me in positions and granting me opportunities—and He kept delivering good things for me—even though I gave Him little in return. I treated Him like He was my genie, there for when I needed Him. He wanted me to give Him my whole heart, but I was keeping that for myself.

Up to that point, I had navigated the seasons of transition in my life from a posture of humility. Entering the league as a rookie, the glitz and glam of the NFL didn't impress me. I felt grateful that God had chosen me to have football as my occupation. Injuries had retired my brother from football. I had played with some mega-talented athletes who didn't play past college—or even finish college. Some squandered their opportunities by not working hard. Others worked hard, did good deeds, and were good people; but for whatever reason, the doors of opportunity never opened for them as they had for me.

Early in my first season, stepping onto the field in a Bears uniform was not about living the NFL life. It was about appreciating the environment I was in.

In high school, I had received autograph requests, but those were from kids in my hometown. In college, as that one reporter discovered, hardly anyone on campus knew who I was. But in the NFL, I was playing on the biggest stage, and playing well. People recognized me in public.

Professional athletes have to be on guard. We work and live under a microscope. The next thing written or said about us could as easily be negative as positive—accurate or not. At the same time, we are constantly elevated. That was especially the case for me in Chicago, where the Bears are deeply loved. I could walk into a restaurant and be ushered to the best table.

"No reservation necessary for you, Mr. Forté."

Strangers paid for my dinner.

For many athletes, the praise feels awkward at first. But after a few times, it becomes customary. And then expected.

I started to wonder what other challenges the sport could give me because of how I had conquered the league as a rookie (or so I thought). If I had accomplished all those records and milestones *as a rookie,* surely I could do that every year.

The humility that had guided me through previous transitions now came under attack. But it was a subtle attack—the kind that crept up on me without my being aware.

I couldn't see how self-confident pride was becoming part of my character.

I had moments when I wondered where that teenager had gone who ducked his head sheepishly when his football accomplishments were mentioned in a Sunday sermon. But I was too spiritually immature to realize that being a reflection of God's glory meant not taking the glory for myself.

As humans, we are not designed to receive glory. God created us to reflect *His* glory. He is the only one who cannot be negatively affected by receiving glory. His character doesn't change. He is worthy of all the honor and praise because He is the Creator of everything. Yet when you look at Jesus' life on earth, He came to *serve.* He could have come as a powerful military leader. Yet, even when those closest to Jesus wanted that from Him, He chose to live in humility. He chose to serve others.

I can now look back and see what I couldn't see then: pride creeping in. My humility slipping. Using my platform for *my own* good. I could score touchdowns and point upward all I wanted, but if I wasn't living to point people to Jesus, what kind of an impact was I having?

Pride is a quiet, subtle evil that even the strongest people are defenseless against without the internal transformation brought by the Holy Spirit. My identity had become caught up in being an NFL running back, and God was working on me to reorient my identity to a point where I would make Jesus my main priority rather than merely an accessory alongside my professional career.

Matthew 6:33 is one of my favorite verses: "Seek first the kingdom of God and his righteousness, and all these things will be provided for you." But I had yet to understand that verse. I had yet to understand that when we place Jesus first in our lives, doubt and worry fade away and are replaced by faith and confidence in a good God regardless of circumstances.

Jesus is the only foundation to build on, and without a rock-solid identity formed on that foundation, it's impossible to know our purpose. At that point in my life, I was chasing personal success. I wish I had known then what I know now: I should have been pursuing significance instead. My NFL success was limited to what I did on the football field and would end when my career ended. Significance carries so much more meaning, and the formula for living with significance is aligning the talents and gifts God has given us with His purpose—which transcends personal preference, professional sports, and even life itself.

I wish I had known how much growth can occur away from the mountaintop, so I would have embraced my time in the valley instead of resisting it. God didn't want me merely to *believe* in Him; He wanted me to make Him Lord over my life. He wanted me to recognize that amid all my striving for success, all I needed was His sufficient grace.

During my second season, I believe the Lord was trying to show me that He is bigger than football. That even though football was a part of me—and He had gifted me with the ability to run the ball—it was not supposed to be my identity.

The hamstring injury was the warning shot I failed to heed.

Playing Hurt

As I worked through the process of rehabbing my injured hamstring, I pressured myself to return as quickly as possible. I knew with the heightened expectations for the upcoming season, my coaches and teammates were counting on me, and Bears fans were counting on me. I had established a high standard my rookie year, and now I needed to go above and beyond that level.

I rushed through the recovery process in order to play at the start of the regular season.

We opened the season with a rebuilt offensive line, and I got off to a slow start, rushing for only 84 yards combined over the first two games, while averaging barely two yards per carry. Jay Cutler also had a rocky start, throwing four interceptions in the first game, a loss to Green Bay. We beat Pittsburgh the following week on the strength of our defense.

In week three in Seattle, I hurt my right knee in the first quarter. I went to the locker room with the trainers to get the knee taped and returned to finish the game. I was later diagnosed with an MCL sprain.

Now I was dealing with injuries to both legs. The hamstring prevented me from running full speed, and the knee sprain limited my lateral movement. That's a hopeless combination. And I couldn't do my regular speed training during the week.

I didn't make excuses to the media, and it would have been a disadvantage to our team for me to talk about my injuries, because of the information it would provide opponents.

I played every game, but I was not the same player as the year before. I should have given my body time to heal. But as a second-year player, I didn't believe I had earned the status—like I thought a veteran would have—to say I needed to sit out and heal. Because I hadn't yet established myself in the league, I felt I was expected to play every game. All it takes is hearing one story about a young player who lost his spot because of an injury to bring job security into the decision-making process.

The fear of gaining a reputation for "always being hurt" was also a factor. Players tagged with the injury-prone label never seem to shed it. I also learned that coaches and training staffs from teams across the league talked to each other to share notes and observations on players. Word would begin to spread that "so-and-so doesn't practice a lot" or "this guy always has problems with his knee." In a league where players constantly change teams through trades, free agency, and getting cut, perception matters.

I noticed early in my career that teams tended to follow a player's lead on injuries. After all, only the player himself could tell how he was really feeling. If he said he could play, his team would put him on the field. Also, the team doctors worked for the team. The goal of rehab was to get the player back on the field as quickly as possible. Sometimes the ability to play the next game took priority over a player's long-term health. The question was always, "Can you play?" If not, it was next man up and the game went on. But if a player believed he was 75 percent, that was a yes. Sixty percent? That could be a yes too. As a player, you wanted to play, even when it was against your better judgment.

As a result of that season, I started seeking outside medical opinions when injured, which the collective bargaining agreement allowed players to do. I believed that by consulting with a medical professional not attached to the team, I would hear a voice speaking on behalf of my health, not my availability to play. That input made me more educated so I could better evaluate when I was ready to return from an injury.

The 2009 season felt like a wash. Despite all the changes we made on offense, the run game struggled. I rushed for 929 yards and totaled 1,400 yards from scrimmage, but my 3.6 yards per carry turned out to be the lowest of my career. Jay threw twenty-six interceptions, and I know he was disappointed after all the excitement surrounding his arrival. Our 7–9 record accurately reflected our season.

When the season ended, I underwent knee surgery to repair a meniscus tear. As part of my rehab, I returned to Fort Lauderdale for speed training with Pete Bommarito, determined to prove that my rookie season was not a fluke. I was sprinting one day and getting close to running at full speed again when I felt another pop in my left hamstring. My immediate fear was that I had reinjured the hamstring and would have to start rehab all over. But a funny thing happened: My hamstring didn't hurt like it had when it popped during OTAs.

I underwent an evaluation and was told that the second pop was the scar tissue breaking apart. I had played the entire season without being fully healed, but now the flexibility in my hamstring returned to normal.

I was physically ready to run like my rookie year again. Spiritually, I needed more work.

13

ONE STEP FROM A SUPER BOWL

The offseason before the 2010 season reminded me of when I was going into my junior year in college. I was now entering the third year of my four-year rookie contract. The third year was the time to establish what type of player I would be in the league. I looked back to my rookie season as my standard.

Staying isolated from voices outside the organization was impossible. Part of the media's job was to write and express their thoughts about the team and me, and Bears fans were vocal with their opinions because of their passion for the team. I could avoid seeking out the various media reports, but what was being written and said would still find its way to me. The Bears had a good public relations department, teammates and coaches might share what they heard, and my family and friends stayed connected to the media.

Ultimately, I couldn't ignore the criticism, but I could use it as fuel. I didn't think my work ethic was in doubt, but my ability certainly was. I was called a "disappointment" because of my second year. Those doubts became the fuel for my offseason workouts.

During that offseason, I came to grips with the fickleness of the fans and the NFL. The same people who tried to crown me as king during my rookie year were now saying I had been overused in 2009 and it was time to find my replacement and prepare him to take over my role.

I responded by upping my training with the help of Andrew Hayes-Stoker, who worked as one of our quality control assistants. Andrew, a former running back at TCU, was a supercool dude who was working his way up in coaching. Because he was just a few years older than me, he could fit in with our players in a role almost between being a player and a coach. But he wasn't like a buddy to the players; he found little ways to challenge us to be better. He still worked out, and because he had played running back, we naturally gravitated to each other.

One day, Andrew got my attention.

"Hey, Forté. You ever see any of the sledding hills around here?"

"We don't sled in Louisiana," I told him. "We don't even have snow."

"You ever run the hills?" he asked.

He reminded me about Walter Payton's well-known offseason conditioning in which he sprinted up steep hills daily to increase his strength and stamina. Andrew told me where I could find hills with different levels of incline and took me to one for my first hill workout.

With my hamstring back to 100 percent, unlike during the previous season, I could focus on training instead of healing. I made sprinting hills part of my workout routine. During OTAs, when our team workouts concluded, I would go run a hill on my own. On one of the shorter hills, I focused on sprint bursts. On the longest hill, where the most difficult part of the workout came near the top, I focused on conditioning.

Entering training camp, I felt like my old self. With our team, though, a lot of new was going on.

In February, Mike Martz was hired as offensive coordinator, replacing Ron Turner. Mike was known for high-scoring, pass-happy offenses. When he was head coach in St. Louis, his Rams had reached the Super Bowl behind their Greatest Show on Turf offense with Kurt Warner as quarterback. In high school, I had watched running back Marshall Faulk play his way into the Hall of Fame as a rusher and receiver in Mike's offense.

Over my ten seasons in the NFL, I played for seven different offensive coordinators. Each change meant learning a new playbook, new philosophies, new blocking schemes, and new terminology. The offenses had the same primary routes, but coordinators gave them different names in their respective systems. Every time a new coordinator came in, it was like going back to my rookie-year camps and OTAs and trying to learn the playbook so I wouldn't have to be thinking about what to do on the field.

Mike's offensive playbook was twice as thick as our previous one, and his terminology was completely different. A flat route is a common route for a running back, and that's typically the route's name because the back's assignment is to run flat to the line of scrimmage. In Mike's offense, that route was called a shoot. Mike also called plays with numbers for the various routes.

In an effort to reinvigorate our running game, Mike Tice was brought in to coach our offensive line. That meant new blocking schemes as well. The same play we had run in previous seasons was blocked differently now. As a back, I needed to learn who was blocking whom, and where, against the defense's flow.

Learning and understanding a new offense required a ton of mental work, and the complexity of Mike Martz's offense required more than usual. The best thing about his offense was it created times when we could line up, see the defense, and expect a big play pre-snap. He built specific details—such as "hot" routes—into his offense. When a defense blitzed, the spot the blitzer came from made a designated receiver the hot read for the quarterback. The difficult part was that we needed to know what every player on the offense would do in each situation. But when the quarterback and hot receiver both made the correct read, a big play would happen.

I also had new competition in camp. In March, the Bears signed veteran running back Chester Taylor to a four-year contract worth $12.5 million, with $7 million guaranteed. Chester, who would turn thirty-one during the summer, had become more of a third-down back in the previous two or three seasons with Minnesota. I didn't understand why the team would pay more than they were paying me to a third-down back, considering I had caught 120 passes over my two seasons. But I learned it's just a fact of life in the NFL that your team is always trying to replace you. It's as if they don't want you to get too comfortable with the position you hold on the team.

During camp, my explosiveness was back to rookie-year level. In our second preseason game, I broke an eighty-nine-yard touchdown run against the Raiders, showing the same breakaway speed as in my first game against the Colts. I knew then that I was in for a special season.

Be Sure Your Sin Will Catch Up with You

Another effect of my growing fame was that old friends and acquaintances were drawn back to me as well. So even though my relationship with Danielle was progressing toward engagement, I reconnected with an ex-girlfriend during a trip to New Orleans for a friend's birthday party, and she ended up getting pregnant.

I couldn't write this book without telling this part of my story. It received some media coverage in Chicago, but I don't think many people outside of those who followed my career with the Bears are aware that this happened.

I think it's important to share my imperfections and brokenness in these pages, because people can idolize professional athletes and overlook our shortcomings. But even though I'm an athlete, I'm no different from anyone else when it comes to the corruption of sin. Though I was raised in the church, I'm still a sinful person who needs to grow in his faith. I've come a long way, but I'm far from perfect.

I encourage Christians to pray for athletes. The lifestyle looks glamorous, but it is filled with temptation, pressure, and failure. At a time when my pride was riding high, and the status I had gained during my rookie season made me feel as if I were untouchable, I violated God's command that sex should only be between husband and wife. I sinned against God, I sinned against Danielle, and I sinned against the way my parents raised me. My son Jaden was born as a result.

I love my son dearly, and I have always been committed to being his father, even though he has grown up in Louisiana with his mother. My sinful actions brought Jaden into the world, but that's not on him. God has a grand plan for Jaden's life.

When the news came to light, Danielle was obviously stunned, and our relationship was hanging in the balance. Fortunately, my story is one of redemption—as it ultimately is for everyone who will repent of their sins. God can redeem anyone, anything, and any situation. We do not have to get ourselves cleaned up before we seek to have a relationship with Jesus. Our uncleanness is the exact reason He gave His life on the cross for us. As it says in 1 John 1:9, "If we confess our sins, [God] is faithful and righteous to forgive us our sins and to cleanse us from all unrighteousness."

I'm not saying it was easy. Danielle and I needed time to work through the damage I had done to our relationship. What I did was traumatic for her and hurt her deeply. I will never try to downplay the pain I caused her. She had every right to say she was done with me. I would not have blamed her one bit. But instead, she forgave me. In the process of restoring our relationship and eventually marrying, I experienced love and forgiveness like never before.

Both of us, however, needed time to work out that forgiveness, and we had to work together to save our relationship.

From my perspective, Danielle's forgiveness mirrored the character of Jesus because she didn't seek revenge or throw me or our relationship away. The faith she demonstrated in that season made me a better man, and I am forever grateful to her. For the first time, I truly saw and understood the full extent of what Jesus did on the cross to wash away our sins and choose to still love us. In Danielle's faith and forgiveness, I saw Jesus.

Danielle and I have been married since 2011, and we have three children together: Nahla, Matthew Christian, and Nia. I admire how Danielle has treated Jaden as one of ours. She sees him no differently than she does Nahla, Matthew, and Nia. She loves all four equally. It takes a strong woman to love that way.

The Bible is clear that we must repent of our sins. Repentance means much, much more than merely admitting a mistake or regretting it. The biblical definition of *repentance* is a change of mind that results in a change of action. It means confessing sin *and* turning away from sin to live in obedience to God. I confessed my sin and committed to living faithfully to Danielle for the rest of my life.

Letdown at Lambeau

In the regular season opener, a 19–14 victory against the division-rival Detroit Lions, I caught seven passes for a career-high 151 yards and two touchdowns. Add in 50 rushing yards, and I gained 201 total yards from scrimmage. Only three times in franchise history had a Bear totaled 200 or more yards in a game.

The first touchdown came on a simple screen pass that I took eighty-nine yards to the end zone. The second was the game-winner with 1:39 to play. On second down from the Lions' 28, Jay threw me a pass along the left sideline that I caught turning to my right and falling backward into the end zone with a hard thud. But I held on to the ball. I owed that play to my teammates, considering I had already had two fumbles (one of which Detroit recovered) and was stopped for no gain on three carries from the Detroit 1 yard line in the fourth quarter.

Our run game, especially early in the season, was not what I hoped it would be. But it was fun to be so involved in the passing game and playing in an offense that could produce a big play at any moment.

Although a Mike Martz offense was known for its emphasis on passing, there was a game in October when we needed to rely on our run game.

At Carolina, a week after we allowed ten sacks in a game against the Giants, two rookies—J'Marcus Webb and Edwin Williams—made their first starts on the offensive line. Jay was out for the game with a concussion, and veteran backup Todd Collins stepped into his place.

We game-planned to run as much as we could.

On our first possession, three of the four plays called were runs. I had a 14-yard run and an 18-yarder for a touchdown. On our next drive, I took the first snap sixty-eight yards for another touchdown that became a footrace to the end zone at about midfield. We defeated the Panthers 23–6 to improve to 4–1 and take over sole possession of first place in the division. I finished with a career-best-to-that-point 166 yards on twenty-two carries. Add in 43 yards from Chester, and we ran for more than 200 yards as a team.

We lost our next two games but then won seven of our next eight, clinching the division title.

Our last game of the regular season was against the Green Bay Packers, the Bears' biggest rival, at historic Lambeau Field. Although we had secured a playoff spot, we had an opportunity to be the number one seed in the NFC and have home-field advantage if we won and Atlanta and New Orleans lost their games.

Hosting playoff games was a great incentive. But for Bears fans, there might have been even more incentive to beat Green Bay: With a loss, the Packers would miss the playoffs. We had defeated them at home 20–17 in week three, so it would have been sweet to know that sweeping the Packers was the reason they stayed home during the postseason.

Bears–Packers is one of the NFL's greatest rivalries, dating to the 1921 game when George Halas's Chicago Staleys defeated Green Bay at Cubs Park.

To me, NFL rivalries are more intense than college football rivalries because, in most cases, NFL rivals are in the same division and play each other twice each season. The stakes are higher for players, too—because we support our families based on our success on the field—especially when a rivalry game is decided by a player's mistake. There's no worse feeling as a player than losing a game against a rival because of your own mistake, and it's a feeling I would not wish on anyone.

The entire city of Chicago fully engaged with the rivalry the week leading up to any Packers game. Soldier Field was at its loudest when the Packers came to town. Even though our stadium was the league's smallest, a Packers game there was much louder than when we played in Green Bay.

I hated playing at Green Bay. Lambeau Field is a historic stadium, but it's old. The tunnel leading onto the field is tiny, and Packers fans would lean over the opening and be right on top of us, shouting all kinds of things at us as we walked out of the tunnel. Good advice was to wear your helmet while walking out of the tunnel.

My wife attended only one game at Green Bay. She sat in the players' wives' section, and Packers fans were staring them down and making rough comments to them. One of the wives was pregnant, and a Packers fan got too rowdy and almost knocked her over. Danielle told me other stories from sitting in the Lambeau stands, too, and after that first experience, she told me she would not be attending any more games in Green Bay. I understood.

I love rivalries. I loved playing in rivalry games and enjoy watching them on TV, in all sports. But I don't like it when people lose perspective in a rivalry. Some players from both sides of the Bears–Packers rivalry who had been around a while had built up disdain for the other team over time. I preferred to separate what happened during games from outside of games. I wanted to play hard, clean football against the other team and then shake hands and hug after the game. After all, it is just a game.

That said, I really wanted to go into Lambeau and ruin the Packers' playoff hopes.

Our game was in the late Sunday afternoon time slot, and the Falcons' and Saints' games were in the early slot. Before kickoff, we knew that both teams had won and that we could not win home-field advantage. I don't know if that hurt our motivation, but our effort just wasn't there from the opening kickoff and we lost 10–3. It's difficult for an NFL team—especially a division champion—to not score a touchdown in sixty minutes, but we managed it.

Walking off the field, I was disappointed because we had missed an opportunity. I hoped it wouldn't come back to bite us later.

Home-Field Advantage

Though we lost home-field advantage throughout the playoffs, we were fortunate to earn a first-round bye. After playing sixteen games over seventeen weeks, the bye was almost like hitting a reset button physically and mentally. We could spend the weekend chilling at home and watching the four teams from each conference in the wild-card round go through an extra round of on-field collisions.

Seattle, which won the NFC West despite having a losing record, upset the defending Super Bowl champion New Orleans Saints 41–36. I hoped the Seahawks would have a bit of an emotional hangover from that game when they came to Soldier Field the following Sunday.

Before our game, the other NFC Divisional Round game took place on Saturday. Top-seeded Atlanta, playing at home, got blitzed 48–21 by . . . the Packers. You want to take it one game at a time in the NFL, and we had not yet played the Seahawks; but the path had been laid out before us: Win the next day and then play the NFC Championship Game *at home*, against Green Bay, with the opportunity to go to the Super Bowl.

Except for the loss in Lambeau, our offense had finished the regular season on a roll. We wanted to jump on Seattle early, take control of the game, and try to get them reflecting early on about what a nice season they'd had with their upset of the defending champs. And we did, scoring on our first possession, again in the first quarter, and adding a third touchdown in the second quarter to take a 21–0 lead into halftime. Our lead grew to 28–0 in the third quarter.

Early in the fourth quarter, with the score 28–3, we had a little fun. Mike sent in a play out of the Wildcat formation, with me lined up at quarterback in the shotgun and Jay split wide right. I faked a handoff to Chester to my left and dropped back to pass. Spotting Devin Hester crossing the middle of the field, right hand raised to indicate he was open, I heaved a pass in his direction. Unfortunately, I failed to spot linebacker Aaron Curry dropping back in zone coverage. He picked off my pass, and I had to go make the tackle on the Seattle sideline.

That was the only pass I threw during my NFL career.

Jay had a good sense of humor laced with sarcasm and a knack for loosening a tense huddle. After I thew the interception, he asked me, "Not as easy as it looks back there, huh?"

We won, 35–24, piling up more than 400 yards of offense. I had 134 total yards, with 80 rushing and 54 receiving on three catches. But I don't think anyone in our locker room believed we had played our best game yet. Still, we were one win from playing in the Super Bowl, and our chance to get there would come down to a game against Green Bay in front of our fans.

We had missed one opportunity to end the Packers' season. The second opportunity would be extra special.

Weather forecasts called for a temperature around twenty degrees with possible snow flurries at opening kickoff. Chicago's weather in the playoffs created the biggest home-field advantage. Green Bay, though, was one of the teams that could come into our house without being bothered by cold weather.

Even as a Louisiana boy, I didn't think cold weather affected my ability to carry the ball—until the temperature dropped into the twenties.

Playing in the cold was all about the hands and feet for me. Keeping a grip on a cold football was difficult. On really cold days, I wore a hand warmer pack around my waist, but with the pouch behind my back. I lined up with my hands behind me and inside the warmer until right before the snap.

We had heated benches, portable heaters, and oversized coats on the sideline. I didn't find any of these to be tremendously helpful. The heaters blew hot air, but I had to be directly in front of them to feel the heat. Besides, whatever warmth I built up on the sideline left as soon as I ran back onto the field and my body temperature dropped. The coats didn't do much other than block the wind. Still, I used all three for every little bit of difference they might make.

I tried to keep my hands and feet warm for as long as possible. Whenever we had the ball during a TV timeout, I ran to the sideline to put on a coat. There was a guy on the sideline who told the officials when the TV broadcast was in a designated commercial break.

He wore long, orange gloves, and he stepped out onto the edge of the field during the timeout and held his gloved hands in the air. The TV commercial breaks lasted about two minutes. When the ads ended, the guy dropped his hands and made a circular motion to let the referee know it was okay to restart play. I watched for that guy to start lowering his orange gloves, and then I dropped my coat and ran back out to the huddle.

In the biggest game of the season, we could not get our offense warmed up. We trailed 14–0 at halftime, and the deficit would have been worse if not for our defense.

Late in the first half, Jay hurt his knee. He started the third quarter, but after we went three-and-out on our first possession, he limped to the sideline and didn't return to the game.

Todd Collins took over at quarterback. He was in the game for two possessions and threw four passes without a completion. Our coaches then made the unusual move of changing to our third-string quarterback, Caleb Hanie. Because he was our designated emergency quarterback for the game, by rule neither Jay nor Todd could come back if Caleb needed to leave the game. Maybe *I* would have played quarterback in that case.

With Caleb in, we finally started moving the ball. I had two runs for first downs on his first drive, and when Chester, in the role of short-yardage back, scored from one yard out, the score was 14–7, and we were suddenly back in the game.

With about six minutes left, the Packers stretched their lead back to fourteen points, at 21–7, on an interception return for a touchdown. We responded by driving for a touchdown on four plays, all completions by Caleb.

Our defense then came up huge again, holding Green Bay without a first down on its next possession and forcing a punt. We took over the ball at our own 29, down by a touchdown, with 2:53 to play and two timeouts left. We probably didn't deserve to be in a position to take the game into overtime based on how we had played, but there we were with that chance. And we started making the most of it.

The Packers' defense was not going to let us get anything deep, but we had plenty of time to methodically work the ball downfield. I caught four passes on the drive, three of which gained first downs, and we crossed the Packers' 30 with 1:15 to go and one timeout left.

However, two plays later, our hopes were dashed and our season ended on a fourth-down interception. We lost 21–14. To the Packers.

Unanswered Questions

Part of being a professional athlete is answering questions from the media. Because of my role on the team, I expected to be interviewed after games and at designated media availability times during the week.

That postgame session was tough.

Of course, the reporters had questions about Jay's injury. I didn't know what had happened to him during the game, other than I saw him limping during his one possession in the third quarter. I wasn't on headsets on the sidelines, so I rarely knew of the conversations that took place during games.

"Y'all have to ask him and the coaches," I told the reporters.

The other questions sought details about the game and my thoughts on our season ending.

I didn't want to talk about the details of losing that game, but I did it because that was how professionals handled defeat. Besides, the majority of interviews were reporters trying to do their jobs to keep fans informed. Our fans wanted to know the answers to most of the questions the reporters were asking. As far as the questions about our season, those were difficult to answer. Fifteen minutes earlier, we were on the field trying to put together a drive to improbably force overtime. Fifteen minutes was not much time to process through all the emotions I was experiencing about the yearlong journey of an NFL season.

What helped in those types of interview settings was feeling like I had at least contributed to the team's chance to win, even though we lost. But a loss of that magnitude, to our most bitter rival, overshadowed a performance I was not ready to evaluate. I had rushed for 70 yards and caught ten passes for 90 yards and a total of 160 yards from scrimmage. The ten receptions broke the Bears' postseason single-game record. Also, only one other Bear had ever gained more than 160 yards from scrimmage in a playoff game, and that had happened way back in 1950.

Context matters in sports. If we had won the game, we would have been headed to the Super Bowl, and I would have been answering questions about my pass-catching ability out of the backfield and the work I had put in over the years to become an every-down back in the NFL. Instead, I stood at my locker trying to answer questions about what had gone wrong.

Both the beauty and the pain of the postseason in any sport is its finality. When teams reach the playoffs, only one will win their final game. The rest, even though they are among the league's best teams, end their season with a loss.

During the regular season, you win a game and say, "Short memory. We're going to enjoy this one tonight, and then tomorrow we'll focus on next week's game." Or after a loss, "It's just one loss. We will reassess, and then it's on to the next one."

But when you lose in the playoffs, you don't move on. You start thinking about all the plays in the game that made a difference. The plays that didn't go your way. The plays the other team made. You regret the plays you didn't make that you could have. Or should have.

The most difficult part is how long you have—the entire offseason—to think about the last game.

On that night, I regretted that we hadn't won the regular season game in Green Bay when we could have prevented the Packers from making the playoffs.

My parents and Danielle's parents attended the playoff game. Usually, we would go to dinner after a game. But I didn't want to have dinner in the city, because whatever restaurant we chose, there would be fans there. I wasn't up to hearing, "But you played well." That didn't matter. We lost. So instead, we went home.

I kept replaying specific plays from the game in my mind. Somebody would say something to me, not even about the game, to try to bring me out of my mental-replay mode. I knew they were trying to help console me, but they probably felt like I was not even there with them.

I recorded every game on TV. Following all the adrenaline surges of a game, it was difficult to fall asleep, so I stayed up late to watch my games after everyone else went to bed.

I did the same that night, too. I watched the whole game, hitting rewind a bunch of times throughout, trying to see what opportunities we failed to take advantage of. I typically muted the announcers to watch our games, but that night, I watched with the sound on. I wanted to hear what the announcers said, curious if they could provide the answers I was searching for.

They couldn't.

I ended my night with the same thought I'd had walking off the field and at my locker and on the ride home. I was sure my teammates were thinking like me too.

We're a good team. We'll improve and be back in the playoffs next year.

Spoiler alert: That was the last playoff game of my career.

14

TAKING CARE OF BUSINESS

The NFL is a business.

As if I needed a reminder, the offseason heading into my fourth year included a lockout by the owners and my own frustrating, drawn-out bid for a contract extension.

When the owners and the NFL Players Association could not agree on a new collective bargaining agreement, the owners declared a lockout in April 2011. That meant the players were barred from entering team facilities, consulting with team doctors, and communicating with coaches.

The lockout finally ended on July 25, and our delayed training camp started four days later.

During the lockout, I was part of a group of Bears players who regularly worked out together at a nearby high school. I practiced playing receiver during those workouts to sharpen my route running for my second year in Mike Martz's offense. I also focused on bulking up in the gym.

A hot topic during the offseason was my contract, because I was entering the fourth and final year of my rookie deal.

Coming off my second 1,000-yard rushing season (1,069) and more than 1,500 yards from scrimmage, my base salary for 2011 was $550,000. Chester Taylor was due $1.25 million for the season, as basically my backup. Then when the lockout ended, the front office signed two other players to contracts that further proved how underpaid I was. First, they signed another running back, Marion Barber, whom the Cowboys had just cut. Marion signed a two-year, $5 million deal. Then we signed punter Adam Podlesh to a five-year contract that paid him about $2 million per year and made him one of the highest-paid punters in the league. Nothing against Adam, who was a nice guy and a good teammate, but if our offense was doing its job, he wouldn't be punting much.

I was making less than the punter and two running backs competing for the spot behind me.

Because of the CBA, the terms of my first contract were essentially predetermined. The key in the NFL is to play your way to a second contract, because that's when you can get paid according to the value you have established for yourself on the field.

By the end of a player's third year in the league, that value is usually set. That's why it is common to see contract extensions after a player's third year in the league. Considering that the average NFL player's career lasts barely three years, players on their second contract are looking for longer-term security. The team also knows that once a player hits free agency and can be signed by any of the other teams, the cost of keeping that player usually skyrockets. In a business where negotiations often get rough, an extension with one year remaining on the rookie contract is typically a win-win for the player and the team.

My salary was so obviously below my performance level that the media had started speculating soon after the 2010 season that I could be in for an extension before the next season. General manager Jerry Angelo said throughout the offseason that signing me to an extension was a priority.

The *H* word—holdout—got thrown around in the media because it was common for a player in my position not to report to training camp, or to at least threaten a holdout, until a new contract was in place. I never intended to hold out because I had a contract I would honor, and I believed holding out would hurt the team.

I reported to training camp in excellent shape to show the value I brought to the team.

With no apparent movement toward an extension from the team, my agent, Adisa, flew in for a face-to-face meeting with general manager Jerry Angelo.

Angelo kept publicly stating that the team would negotiate with me in good faith. Looking back, I dislike his comments, because anyone who uses the words *good faith* should be a man of his word and tell the truth about the situation. The film and stats were telling the truth that I had far outperformed my rookie contract. Most teams that value their top performers want to keep those players around through a contract extension.

Angelo offered a contract comparable to what Jamaal Charles was making with Kansas City—a little more than $6 million per year sharing the backfield with Thomas Jones. As a full-time starter, I saw it as a lowball offer.

In the NFL, agents handle negotiations with the team, but I did meet once with Angelo and Adisa. The Bears' offer was not even top fifteen in the league, and I wanted to hear the GM attempt to make sense of his offer.

Adisa presented a compelling case that a more accurate comparison than Jamaal Charles was Adrian Peterson of the Vikings. Adisa showed my statistical similarities to Adrian's first three years. Adrian and Tennessee's Chris Johnson, a member of my draft class, were also in the process of negotiating new contracts expected to be much larger than what I had been offered. (Both signed new deals that September, Adrian for an average of $14 million per year and Chris—who held out during training camp—for $13 million per year.)

The only defense Angelo made for his offer was that I hadn't yet made a Pro Bowl appearance. A vote of players and fans select the Pro Bowl teams. Players don't vote on every position because they don't have time during the season to evaluate each position. The Pro Bowl was a great honor to receive, and an individual goal that players pursued, sometimes even negotiating Pro Bowl bonuses into their contracts. But making the Pro Bowl, to some degree, was a popularity contest.

I turned down the Bears' offer and decided to play out my rookie contract, as underpaid as I was, and use free agency as leverage for a contract in line with what I had earned.

The opportunity in that situation was to allow God to refine my character instead of folding my arms and pouting. It was another reminder that money was not everything, and that I needed to trust that I would be paid what God wanted me to be paid, in His timing. I also learned the importance of knowing my value and not settling for less, believing God had a perfect plan for my future.

In Prime Position

We opened the season at home against Atlanta, and I started that game on fire. I caught three passes on our first possession that moved us into position for a Robbie Gould field goal. Two possessions later, on a first down from our own 44, I caught a screen pass off a fake reverse behind the line of scrimmage. I had three blockers ahead of me who made their blocks perfectly. I made the safety miss at the Falcons' 45, absorbed a hit at the 35 that knocked me momentarily off balance, regained my footing, and won another footrace to the end zone.

I did my usual touchdown celebration ending with a point heavenward, and after seeing fans behind the end zone wearing "Pay Forté" T-shirts, I added an extra touch: the Michael Jordan shrug to ask our general manager, "What else do y'all want me to do to believe that I can be your running back?"

The funny thing about that touchdown was that Tyler Clutts came in at fullback on that play to give the defense a run look on first down. That was Tyler's first game in the league. He was undrafted out of Fresno State and had played in the Canadian Football League, the Arena Football League, and the United Football League before the Cleveland Browns picked him up late in the 2010 season and placed him on their practice squad. The Browns released him the week before the first game and signed him back to their practice squad. Players on one team's practice squad can be signed by another team as long as that team puts the player on its active fifty-three-man roster. The Bears picked him up on Wednesday, four days before the Atlanta game.

Imagine trying to learn special teams and enough of a new playbook to play in a game that quickly, much less a Mike Martz playbook.

When Jay gave us the play, I could tell from Tyler's facial expression that he was confused. As we broke the huddle, Tyler said, "Jay, Jay! What do I do?" Jay didn't answer, probably because he was already starting to look over the defense's alignment. On this play, Jay was under center, I was lined up seven yards behind him, and Tyler was offset to my right. As we stepped into our places, Tyler looked over his right shoulder to me and asked, "What do I do?"

"Run a wheel route and block whoever is out there," I told him.

We snapped the ball, and Tyler ran a wheel route. When he got to the line of scrimmage, he turned back toward the backfield like he was lost. As I caught the pass from Jay on the numbers, Tyler spun to his left, stumbled, and regained his balance to go block whoever he could find in a white jersey. As it turned out, he made the block that really sprung me.

I later told Tyler that when he asked me what to do, I was trying to figure out what I should do as well because we hadn't practiced that play out of that formation.

Here we had made this big play, and it was almost as if we were drawing it up in the dirt at John Slidell Park instead of against an opponent on an NFL field.

In the following two weeks, I caught ten passes for 117 yards against New Orleans and seven passes for 80 yards against the Packers. I had more than twice as many yards receiving as I did rushing through the first three games.

Then our run game started clicking.

Over the next five games, I rushed for 205 yards against Carolina, 116 against Detroit, 87 against Minnesota, 145 against Tampa Bay, and 133 against Philadelphia. Eight games into the season, I led the NFL in yards from scrimmage (1,241) and was second in rushing (805). The Philly game in that stretch was the third in a five-game winning streak that improved our record to 7–4 and placed us in the thick of the fight for a wild-card berth with five games to play.

During the final game of that winning streak, however, Jay broke the thumb on his passing hand while making a tackle and needed surgery, which knocked him out for the rest of the year.

Another Box Checked

The concern—the risk—when an athlete turns down a new contract like I did is that an injury would harm the next round of negotiations. We lost our first game without Jay and played Kansas City desperately in need of a win to stay in the playoff hunt. I entered that game fifteen yards shy of my third 1,000-yard rushing season.

But I didn't get there.

Midway through the first quarter, we called a counter play to the left. At the line of scrimmage, I spotted the safety positioned far to the right. If everyone made their blocks, I would be staring at a long stretch of lush, green grass, and we would soon be celebrating a ninety-two-yard touchdown run.

The tight end went in motion to the right and set up behind the right tackle. As I took the handoff from Caleb, the right guard pulled to kick out the outside linebacker, and the tight end came back left to take on the play-side inside backer. He was supposed to wrap around to make his block, but the defense had shifted, and he went too wide and missed his man. As a running back, I had to anticipate that blocks would be made. At the speed of the game, holes could open and close in fractions of a second. If I waited for that hole to open, I would have missed my opportunity.

Derrick Johnson was the Chiefs' linebacker who slipped underneath the block. He dove, and his helmet hit directly on my right knee. My knee buckled as he knocked both feet out from under me. I heard a collective gasp from the crowd. When I rolled over and clutched my knee, the stadium went silent.

After the trainers checked me on the field, I was able to walk to the trainer's table on the sideline. They examined my knee further and diagnosed a sprained MCL. If the diagnosis was confirmed by an MRI the next day, my season would be over.

While the game continued without me, I went to the locker room to change into my street clothes, feeling an odd sense of relief. Even after not getting the extension I wanted, I had played to finish out my rookie contract without complaining. I was among the league leaders in rushing yards and total yards, so my effort could not be questioned. I had done all I could to prove my value to the team. Though I would miss the final four games of the season, I would recover fully from this injury.

As I was removing my pads in the locker room, I heard a knock on the back door. I had no idea who would have access to that area during the game, but I limped over to the door and cracked it open. Outside was Danielle, with tears streaming down her cheeks.

"Girl, why are you crying?" I asked.

"You were down on the field, and you didn't get up," Danielle said. "I thought you were really hurt."

"Yeah, I sprained my MCL," I told her. "I'm probably going to be out the rest of the season. But guess what? I'm still here. On the large scale of things, this is just a game, even though this is what I do for a living."

I dried her cheeks, hugged her, and assured her I was okay.

We lost that game to the Chiefs and the next three before beating Minnesota in the finale for an 8–8 finish. I ended up with 997 yards rushing and 1,397 total yards.

The week of the final game, I was named one of five Bears selected to the Pro Bowl, along with Brian Urlacher, Lance Briggs, Peanut Tillman, and Corey Graham. Jerry Angelo had told me that the one thing I hadn't done to earn a better contract was to make the Pro Bowl. Now I had checked that box, as well, and I was ready to talk contract again.

Answering the Call

If I plotted out my faith journey as a line graph, there would be a noticeable rise after the 2011 season. I attribute that uptick to the arrival in Chicago of quarterback Josh McCown.

If you look up our team stats from that year, you'll see that Josh passed for 414 yards and two touchdowns. Not much in the scope of a season. But what I remember most about Josh from that year was the role he played in changing my life.

Because of Jay Cutler's injury, Josh joined our team the day before Thanksgiving as an experienced backup to our new starter, Caleb

Hanie. Josh had come into the league in 2002 and previously played in Mike Martz's offense. Though he hadn't played in an NFL game since 2009—having spent the 2010 season in the United Football League—Josh provided a needed veteran presence behind Caleb.

That's the football side of Josh. But it was the personal side that had the greatest impact on me.

Because Josh arrived in Chicago alone, ahead of his wife and children, Danielle and I invited him to our place for Thanksgiving. Beginning with that meal, and as I got to know him over the rest of the season, Josh became a source of encouragement to me. We participated in Bible studies together, and he added biblical knowledge and spiritual maturity to our group. His ability to quote from the Bible inspired me to want to memorize Scripture. I also admired how public he was with his faith without being pushy. It was easy to see that Josh lived out his Christianity every day, in all settings.

Teammate by teammate, he worked his way around the locker room with invitations to attend an offseason conference in Orlando, Florida, hosted by a ministry called Pro Athletes Outreach, or PAO. If a player and his wife, fiancée, or girlfriend wanted to go, Josh told them he would cover their expenses. I was among eight or nine guys who committed to go, and Josh paid the way for every one of us.

When I told Danielle about PAO, she said she had heard from wives of players from other teams that it was a helpful conference. I didn't have very high expectations, but I figured, if nothing else, I would enjoy a free trip to Orlando with my wife.

When we arrived at the conference, I was still skeptical about whether the time would be beneficial.

The first speaker was pastor Tony Evans. When he started talking, I was sitting back in my chair, arms folded. Three minutes later, I was writing all kinds of notes, trying to keep up with all the wisdom he was dropping on us. As he continued to speak, I felt a growing conviction that I was not living the life God designed for me.

During the conference, I enjoyed being in a spiritual environment with other professional athletes. There was nobody asking for autographs, or money, or for us to do anything else for them. We were all peers.

One challenge for believers in the NFL is the lack of a true faith community. Football dominates a player's calendar and his thinking throughout the season. With most games on Sunday, it was difficult to attend a local church. Most players don't have a local church in the city where they play because their permanent home is elsewhere. Even when the schedule allows time for attending a church on a Sunday morning, players who are recognized in public cannot just walk into any church and be like everybody else. To try to compensate, there are chaplains and team chapels and player-led Bible studies during the week, but the committed and caring community that is one of the chief functions of the local church is largely missing.

Danielle and I were pleasantly surprised to experience that sense of community during the conference.

Other speakers described what it looks like to serve God authentically instead of playing a starring role in the story. I was fascinated by the sight of big, powerful, athletic football players kneeling on the floor, raising their hands, and submitting their lives to Christ. What I observed reached far below the surface-level, perfunctory religious routines in my life.

The conference challenged me to be authentic and to realize that faith was deeper than the mere lip service of saying that Jesus is my Lord and Savior in a postgame interview.

As we're told in James 1:22, "Be doers of the word and not hearers only, deceiving yourselves." I realized I had been a *hearer* only, deceiving myself into thinking I was good because I was faithful in attending pregame chapel and a weekly Bible study and praying before games. But that was my only *doing*. I had the foundation of

Jesus in my life, and I'd had it as far back as I could remember, but I couldn't point to much I had built on that foundation.

Elsewhere in the New Testament, the apostle Paul writes about the need for believers to grow from babies in Christ, who drink milk, into mature believers who live on solid food. Paul told the believers in his day that they were not growing spiritually because they were "still worldly."[2]

The conference became a turning point in my faith because it opened my eyes to the need for a deeper relationship with Jesus. It also started me on a path to thinking about making better use of my platform, which led me to create the What's Your Forté Foundation.

Back home, as I reflected on the conference, I began thinking about what good was coming out of people knowing my name and knowing me as a Pro Bowl running back. I never forgot that an NFL career could be gone in an instant, but I had never seriously considered what people would think of me after my playing days other than, "He was a good running back." I asked myself, *What will people remember after they've met you? What will they say you did for them?*

Though I had used the platform God provided me to say I was a Christian and to give Him the glory in interviews and champion Jesus' name, I realized I couldn't name what I was doing tangibly to actually change people's lives.

The murder of Brandon Spincer, my Tulane teammate, had stayed in my mind because of how often gun violence made the news in Chicago. Over my four seasons with the Bears, I had learned about how complex the realities of life were in parts of the city, especially in neighborhoods on the south and west sides. Children lacked educational resources because of the zip codes they were born into. I heard stories of students entering high school at a third-grade reading level.

---

[2] 1 Corinthians 3:3.

The number of incarcerated teens was stunning. I could not help but wonder how my life might have turned out if I had been born into one of those neighborhoods.

I asked myself some pointed questions.

Why has God given you this platform? Are you here to make money or to make a difference?

I decided to use my platform to actually do something to help people change their lives. I began working to establish a foundation built around my name to focus on gun violence prevention through education and resources. Just like I'd had to be exposed to the game of football before I fell in love with the sport, I wanted my foundation to expose the youth in some of Chicago's most troubled neighborhoods to career opportunities that were not being placed in front of them.

The What's Your Forté Foundation officially launched in 2013. It's still going strong, and I have been able to invest even more of my time into the work since my retirement. I will share more about that work and some of our success stories later. But the origin of the foundation—finding a purpose to fulfill—started during the 2011 offseason with one teammate, Josh McCown, paying it forward for Danielle and me to attend the PAO conference. I know Josh would tell you that he invited us out of obedience to the Lord, who put it on his heart to influence others.

It's easy to look for ways to change the world while missing opportunities to change the corner of the world we live in. It doesn't matter whether our sphere of influence is large, small, or somewhere in between; what matters is what we do with what God has called us to do.

The What's Your Forté Foundation is an example of how, when we answer God's call and go to work, He produces results.

15

BIG DECISIONS

The day after the 2011 season ended, Bears president Ted Phillips fired general manager Jerry Angelo, and Mike Martz resigned as offensive coordinator because of "philosophical differences" with head coach Lovie Smith.

A few days later, offensive line coach Mike Tice was promoted to offensive coordinator. In late January, Phil Emery was hired to replace Jerry Angelo as GM. Emery was the Chiefs' director of college scouting and had previously worked for the Bears as a scout. The following day, I played in the Pro Bowl on a limited basis. My knee injury had healed, and the Bears' medical staff cleared me to play, but I played only in the second quarter, rushing twice for six yards and catching a four-yard pass from New Orleans quarterback Drew Brees.

Under the collective bargaining agreement, teams can place what is called a franchise tag on one player whose contract is expiring and could become a free agent. When a player received the franchise tag, he was given a one-year contract based on the top five salaries in the league at his position. But the player and the team could still negotiate and come to an agreement on a new contract while the franchise tag was in place. The NFL sets a date each year for when its official new year begins. On that date, free agents can start signing with teams. That offseason, the NFL year began on March 13. The deadline for teams to designate franchise players was March 5.

Three days before the franchise tag deadline, Phil Emery announced that I had been designated as the Bears' franchise player, meaning I would receive a salary of $7.7 million for the upcoming season if I signed what was known as a franchise tender. I didn't immediately sign the tender. Later that month, the team signed free agent running back Michael Bush to a four-year contract. Though I didn't like that the Bears always seemed to be trying to find my replacement, I recognized that was part of the business and the way good teams operated. Still, the way the Bears went about bringing in running backs always made it feel like they were trying to get rid of me. This time, signing a running back to a *four-year* contract before resolving my status was a slap in the face. By tying me up with the franchise tag, the front office was telling me that securing me to a longer-term deal was not their top priority.

When April OTAs rolled around, I still hadn't signed the franchise tender. I couldn't practice, but I worked out with Pete Bommarito in Fort Lauderdale. That was one of the healthiest offseasons of my career.

Adisa held conversations with the Bears front office about a long-term contract extension, but it felt like they were trying to guilt us into accepting the one-year tender offer. They were saying that the general manager was new and that they wanted me to sign so I could attend OTAs to learn the new playbook and be around my teammates. But a contract extension would have accomplished the same purpose while giving me some security. To an outsider, $7.7 million for one year and the opportunity to keep negotiating on a new contract probably sounds good. But once that franchise tender was signed, the team would have no incentive to discuss a new deal. Meanwhile, I would have to play another season—risking an injury that could end my career or harm my leverage in negotiating my next contract—in order to get to a multiyear contract with some possible guarantees.

As players, we gave a ton of ourselves to the game, but the question was always what the game would give us in return. We knew that the business of football would use us up and move on to the next guy.

I wanted financial security for my family, and I had no problem expressing publicly my frustration over the lack of progress toward a long-term deal.

The deadline to sign the franchise tender was Monday, July 16. As the deadline neared, I remained optimistic that we would reach an agreement.

I had hoped to sign a five-year contract, but the Bears offered only four. We agreed to that, but the Bears included injury provisions—basically, exclusions if I got hurt—even though I had missed only four games over my first four years. If I didn't dress for a game because of injury, I wouldn't receive a portion of a bonus that—considering the size of the contract we were negotiating—amounted to pennies on the dollar for the team. According to my agent, no other Bears player had that provision written into his contract.

I initially balked at signing because of the injury clause. Adisa said he didn't like that part of the contract either, but pointed to my history of durability. He said if I felt strongly enough to fight its inclusion, I could talk with the general manager face-to-face.

I visited with Phil Emery and brought up the injury provision.

"That's what's hanging this up," I told him. "Why are y'all putting that in the contract for me when it's not in the contract of anyone else who has had injuries and missed more games than me?"

"Well," Phil answered, "if you don't miss games, you don't have anything to worry about."

"Just so you know," I said, "my leg could be broken off, and I'm going to dress for the game just to get the bonus."

"That's fine with me," he said.

Adisa did a great job representing me, and on the day of the deadline, I signed a four-year contract for almost $32 million. Importantly, $17.1 million was guaranteed. Even if the Bears cut me the next day, I would receive the guaranteed amount. That was the financial security I wanted for my family. I thanked God for repeatedly assuring me after I received the lowball offer the year before that I would eventually receive what He had planned for me.

I disliked contract negotiations because of the silly stuff that always seemed to come up (like the injury provision only for me) and because of their potential to damage relationships. But that's how teams in the NFL did business.

Overall, I was pleased with the contract. I would have liked a fifth year, but I was convinced I would play all four years and sign a third contract—an opportunity that comparatively few NFL players get.

Touchdown to Remember

With the off-field business done, and the security of a new contract in place, my motivation going into the season was to prove I deserved that contract. I didn't want to be one of those players of whom it could be said, "Once he got the big paycheck, his performance fell off."

By my fifth season, a shift was taking place within the league. The NFL today is a passing league, and I sensed a transition to that style of play beginning around the 2012 season.

Offenses were starting to feature more run-pass options. Jay Cutler was not a running quarterback, so we played more of a Spread-type offense and ran out of the shotgun. Also, defensive coordinators now knew I was a receiving threat out of the backfield. Blitzing became a way of removing that threat because it forced me to stay in the backfield to block. They knew my tendencies and game-planned for the play calls that best suited my game.

Great players, once they have been studied on film like I had, find new ways to be successful. That became my challenge at that stage of my career.

We opened the season at home against Indianapolis. It was our first time playing the Colts since my NFL debut and our third consecutive year to open the season at home. There was no better place to kick off a new season than at Soldier Field. All the expectations and hope that fans had stored up for the new season would be on display, and the Chicago weather in early September was hard to beat.

I gave my parents two complimentary tickets for the game. When I went out to the field for pregame warm-ups, I was surprised to see that their seats were better than usual. Much better, in fact. Mom and Dad were seated in the front row behind one of the end zones.

All right! First game of the season. In Soldier Field. Parents in the front row. I don't know if I'll ever have this opportunity again. I've got to score in that end zone.

Our first possession had us moving toward my parents' seats. Jay got sacked on our 4 yard line on the first play, and we followed that with a false start. I ran for a short gain on the next play, and after an incompletion following a bad snap, we had to punt.

The Colts had selected quarterback Andrew Luck of Stanford with the first overall pick in the draft, and there was a lot of hype about his first NFL start. Our defense held Luck and the Colts without a first down on their first possession. The ensuing punt pinned us at our own 3 yard line.

On our first play, Jay threw a short pass to me out to the right.

Jerrell Freeman, the linebacker to that side, undercut my route, picked off the pass at the four, and returned it for a touchdown. The Colts were playing a single-high safety on the play, and Brandon Marshall, our receiver to the right, dragged his corner toward the middle of the field. There was a whole lot of green grass in front of me. If Jay had lofted the ball over the backer, the next person to touch me probably would have been one of my parents reaching over the wall to hug me.

Following the kickoff, we went on a long drive—still toward my parents—into Indianapolis territory. On second-and-ten at the Colts' 16, I carried the ball to the 1. I wanted the ball again to finish off the drive. We passed on first down, and the Colts were called for pass interference. I looked to the sideline and saw Michael Bush jogging toward the huddle. Michael was the latest running-back-over-my-shoulder the team had signed. His role was short yardage back. I never wanted to come out of any game with the ball that close to the goal line, but especially with my parents sitting in that end zone. I retreated to the sideline and watched as Michael carried the ball on the next two plays and scored.

My next opportunity to score in front of Mom and Dad came in the third quarter. We led 24–14 and had a first down at the Indy 12. I carried the ball up the middle to the 6, and then got the ball on the next play as well. I took the handoff to Jay's right, didn't see room there, stutter-stepped to buy the linemen more time, and saw a crease forming to my left. I shot through the hole, stepped through an arm tackle, and lowered my shoulders to slip between two defenders and into the end zone. I stood up, did my usual touchdown celebration, and ran over to where my parents were standing and cheering. I pointed to them with both hands and handed the ball up to my dad. I could see the joy on their faces as Dad reached over the railing and patted me on the top of my helmet.

I kept the ball from every touchdown in my career and had each one painted as a memento. Except for that one ball. My parents still have it. A photographer snapped a photo the moment I handed the ball to my dad, and that picture hangs in my home gym today.

That enhanced touchdown celebration remains one of my favorite memories from my career because of what the moment represented: My dad getting up and going to work for Shell all those years and making it home in time to practice with Bryan and me. My mom throwing balls and shooting hoops outside with us. My dad's football career, and the countless hours he spent coaching my teams, investing his time to help me become a good football player and a good man.

And then to score a touchdown the one time they sat behind the end zone gave me the opportunity to hand them the football as a way of saying thank you, as their son, for all they had poured into me.

Needless Change?

We took care of Indianapolis, 41–21, and moved on to week two—a showdown with the Packers at Lambeau Field on *Thursday Night Football.* We trailed at halftime, 13–0, and had gained less than fifty yards on offense. We started the third quarter with the ball and were determined to put together a scoring drive. I touched the ball on the first four plays, three carries and a catch for a first down.

After an incompletion, Jay checked down to me on third-and-nine. With Charles Woodson in pursuit, I passed the first down marker along our sideline. Charles grabbed me from behind and brought me down with a hip-drop tackle—a maneuver that the NFL began penalizing starting with the 2024 season. My right ankle got caught underneath and rolled over. I got up right away but stayed on the sideline so the trainers could look at me. I had sprained my ankle and didn't return to the game, which we lost, 23–10.

I hadn't suffered a high ankle sprain, which is more severe than a classic ankle sprain, but I couldn't practice during the week and was on the inactive list for a home game against the St. Louis Rams. Of course that meant I was forced to be in street clothes on the sideline instead of dressing out, and that cost me bonus money.

We beat the Rams to improve to 2–1, and the following week's game was against the Dallas Cowboys on *Monday Night Football.* With the extra day off, I hoped to be able to play. I practiced on a limited basis during the week, and by Saturday I could sprint and cut—though I was listed as questionable on the team's injury report. The ankle still hurt, even when something just brushed up against it.

It was one thing to take part in a practice, but that was nothing like a game. I always wanted to make my first contact in a game as quickly as I could. Coming back from an injury, I wanted to give the injured body part a test as soon as possible.

Our first play was a handoff to me. I made a couple moves in the backfield without issue and then sliced through a hole for a gain of eight yards. On the tackle, I wound up at the bottom of a pile of six or seven guys. My ankle got pinned under a lot of weight. Pain shot through my body. I got up and limped off the field. A trainer checked on me, and I said the ankle was fine. But it hurt like crazy. I got my ankle retaped for better support and was back on the field before the drive ended.

Fortunately, we never trailed during the game, and I could take most of the fourth quarter off.

That was one of those games when I decided to fight through the pain because I wanted to prove that I was worth the money in my new contract. But it was also one of those games when I was asking myself, *Should I really be out here?*

With our 34–18 win on the road in front of a national TV audience, we announced our intention to return to the playoffs. Then we backed up that statement with five more wins in a row.

Halfway through our schedule, we were 7–1 and sitting atop the NFC North, a game and a half ahead of Green Bay. We endured a two-game mini-slide when Jay suffered a concussion, and we were tied with the Packers at 7–3 with three of our next four games at home.

We beat Minnesota the first week, followed by an overtime loss to Seattle and rookie quarterback Russell Wilson, who was running all over the field making plays against our defense. Then came the two games that wound up dooming our season: a loss at Minnesota (21–14) and another loss at home against Green Bay (21–13).

With two road games remaining, we were not out of the playoff picture, but we had to win out and hope for some help. We got our two wins (against Arizona and Detroit), but we didn't get the help we needed.

Our season ended in front of the TV as we watched the Vikings kick a field goal on the final play of the game to defeat the Packers. Despite our 7–1 start, we finished 10–6, one game behind Green Bay in the division and tied with Minnesota for second place. Our two losses to the Vikings gave them the tiebreaker and a wild-card spot. We had failed to take care of business against Green Bay and Minnesota, and it proved costly.

We not only missed the playoffs, but our coach lost his job.

On New Year's Eve, less than twenty-four hours after our season ended, Lovie Smith was fired.

When I heard the news, I was shocked. There had been speculation that Lovie's time with the Bears might be running out, but he had coached us to ten wins. Yes, we missed the playoffs, but winning ten games in the NFL isn't easy. Over the nine seasons that Lovie coached the Bears, we won 56 percent of our games. He had led the Bears to the Super Bowl and was one win from doing it a second time after the 2010 season.

Lovie addressed the team that morning. It was pretty emotional. Defense was Lovie's specialty, and the defensive players were noticeably upset. The offensive guys supported Lovie too.

I didn't understand the move. We hadn't developed a consistent offense under Lovie, but we were close to being a playoff-level team. And our defense was already there. Actually, we had a championship-level defense, with several veterans who were perennial Pro Bowl players and possible future Hall of Famers. The windows for winning don't stay open long in the NFL, because of player turnover and the salary cap, but our veterans still had fuel in the tank. Why disrupt that continuity? Bringing in a new head coach, and the changes that would mean for the defense, made no sense.

I loved watching Lovie coach the defense during practices. He held them to a high standard every day. Every defensive coach emphasizes creating turnovers, but Lovie went a step further and said he wanted our defense to score points. And our special teams, too.

The only explanation I could come up with for firing Lovie was that the fans had grown tired of him, and the decision-makers in the front office listened to the fans.

You've heard the old expression, "Be careful what you wish for"? When Bears management fired Lovie, I feared they were wishing for something they wouldn't want.

16

THE SEASON EVERYTHING CHANGED

The weekend of the conference championship games, the Bears made an atypical hire in selecting Marc Trestman as the head coach to replace Lovie Smith. Trestman had been coaching in the Canadian Football League for the past five seasons.

Trestman had had success in Canada, leading the Montreal Alouettes to two Grey Cup championships. He was an offensive-minded coach widely known for his work developing quarterbacks.

Before going to the CFL, Trestman had been offensive coordinator in Cleveland, San Francisco, Arizona, and Oakland, plus at the collegiate level at North Carolina State. His schemes featured a heavy influence from the West Coast offense, a ball-control philosophy built around short passes. Running backs tended to play a more significant role in the passing game in a West Coast offense.

Trestman also came to the Bears with the reputation of being an intelligent guy. He had graduated from law school and practiced law during a break from coaching. He had also authored a book on leadership and teamwork.

Though Trestman would call the plays on offense, he also hired Aaron Kromer from New Orleans as offensive coordinator. When Kromer came to Chicago, he told me that the Saints had been "this close" to drafting me in 2008, but they decided to keep seven-year veteran Deuce McAllister, even though he had missed most of the previous year with an injury. The 2008 season had turned out to be Deuce's last in the league, and Aaron told me, "We could have used you." So I had been close—*this close*—to playing in New Orleans.

The Bears' offseason moves made it clear that management was focused on improving our offense. Since my rookie season, we had drafted only one offensive lineman earlier than the seventh round. In 2013, we took two, starting with Kyle Long of Oregon with our first pick, at number twenty. In the fifth round, we chose Jordan Mills from Louisiana Tech. We also added an offensive lineman through free agency, awarding the richest contract for a lineman in Bears' history to left tackle Jermon Bushrod, who had played for Kromer with the Saints. All three additions wound up starting every game for us that season.

A new coaching staff meant that, going into my sixth season, I would be playing for my fifth offensive coordinator, with another brand-new playbook and terminology to learn.

Fortunately, I only had to learn Trestman's new offense. With five years' experience in the league, I understood defensive coverages, route concepts, and what offensive coaches wanted to do to create a numbers advantage in the run game and one-on-one mismatches in the passing game.

With the move to a West Coast offense, I knew the number of opportunities I would receive as an every-down back would hinge on learning more of the intricacies of the new passing game. Early in my career, my success as a receiver came from my speed and hands. Our play callers would look to get me one-on-one against a linebacker, and I would outrun him for a deep ball. Or near the goal line, they would throw me a back-shoulder fade and let my hands do the work.

Jay would be throwing more short passes in this offense, so I worked on my route-running by watching how wide receivers ran slants. This way, I could give Jay more options by lining up in the slot. I had started that process at least a year earlier after deciding it needed to be the next step in my development as a running back. With the new offense, I expected that work would immediately reap dividends.

Coming out of training camp, I loved how we had upgraded our offense. The three new linemen, combined with veteran center Roberto Garza and left guard Matt Slauson, gave us probably the best offensive line I ran behind. Brandon Marshall and Alshon Jeffery were back as receivers, with Alshon showing big-play ability going into his second season.

We also had the advantage to start the season without opponents having film of our new offense. As we continued to install additional sections of the playbook as the season progressed, our opponents' defensive game plans looked like they were trying to play catch-up to all our changes.

As a result, an offense that had finished in the middle of the pack the previous season by scoring 23.4 points per game, started the season by scoring, in succession, 24, 31, 40, and 32 points over the first four games. Unfortunately, the new defense was not playing up to the standard of recent seasons. We were 3–1 after those four games, but we had won one game by three points and another by one point. In the game where we scored 32 points, we allowed 40 and lost.

With two games remaining in the regular season, our 8–6 record had us atop the NFC North, half a game ahead of Green Bay and one up on Minnesota. If we won our games at Philadelphia and at home against the Packers to finish the season, we would be division champions regardless of how any other teams fared.

Instead, we got steamrolled in Philly, 54–11, in front of a national TV audience on *Sunday Night Football.* The Eagles scored 21 points in the first quarter, and we didn't score a touchdown until the last play of the third quarter. Fortunately, earlier in the day, Green Bay and Detroit both lost their games, eliminating the Lions from playoff contention and setting up our season finale against the Packers, at Soldier Field, as a game to determine which team would make the playoffs.

In the NFL, you have to take care of business when you have the opportunity. We didn't in Philadelphia, and we failed to do so again against the Packers, despite being given a second chance at home.

We scored first on a four-yard pass from Jay to me late in the first quarter. Green Bay came back in the second quarter with two field goals and a defensive touchdown on a fumble return, and we trailed 13–7 at halftime.

We regained the lead on our first drive of the second half on my five-yard touchdown run. In typical Bears–Packers fashion, Green Bay scored a few minutes later to go in front 20–14. We answered on our next drive, and my one-yard run—my third touchdown of the game—put us in front again at 21–20. Jay and Brandon hooked up for a short scoring pass on the first play of the fourth quarter to increase our lead to 28–20. The Packers then scored on their next possession, and we led 28–27 with 11:38 to play.

The game had become an exchange of quick-strike touchdowns, and we wanted to eat some clock after Green Bay's kickoff. We moved the ball into Packers' territory and killed more than five minutes before punting to the Green Bay 13.

Then Aaron Rodgers, in his first game back from a broken collarbone, did what Aaron Rodgers made a career of doing: He led his offense on a game-winning drive.

Even on that drive, we had opportunities we failed to take advantage of. Three times, the Packers faced fourth down. They converted all three, and the third conversion ended our season when, on fourth-and-eight from our 48, Rodgers hit Randall Cobb for a long touchdown pass. We lost 33–28 to miss the playoffs for the fifth time in my six years.

We had gone from being a team with a strong defense and an offense that struggled to find consistency to having the league's second-highest scoring offense, scoring more points than any Bears team since the 1985 team that won the Super Bowl.

The new offense suited me well, as I rushed for 1,339 yards—second-best in the NFL behind the Eagles' LeSean McCoy—and averaged 4.6 yards per carry. Over my ten-year career, that season was my highest rushing total for any year and my second-best yards-per-rush average. I also caught seventy-four passes for 594 yards—both career highs to that point. My 1,933 total yards from scrimmage set another career high.

The league's players and fans voted me into my second Pro Bowl. I credit my first Pro Bowl selection to our offensive line coach at the time, Mike Tice. I believe my second selection resulted from my consistency as both a rusher and a receiver.

Though we fell short of making the playoffs in 2013, we had become a completely different team—one that would have to rely on its offense to win games. I welcomed that opportunity for our offensive unit. But with the coaching change, the team culture had also changed. The differences weren't showing up in the league standings yet.

But they would.

Getting Serious About My Faith

In sports, it's common to hear players go into an offseason talking about "unfinished business" from the just-concluded season.

My offseason included some unfinished *spiritual* business, as well.

After the experience Danielle and I had at the Pro Athletes Outreach conference in 2012, we wanted to attend the following year. But our daughter, Nahla, was born in 2013. So we made sure we attended in early 2014.

I grew up a believer and told people I was a Christian. But when asked today about when I made a decision to give my life to Jesus Christ, I say it was at the 2014 PAO conference. I had believed in Jesus, but I hadn't been following Him. That changed at the conference.

After the first conference, I continued attending the weekly chapels and the players' Bible study. The chaplain started a couples' Bible study within the team, and Danielle and I attended. I was back to living out my faith through routines, back to doing good things—but not much more.

During the 2014 conference, a heavy burden of hypocrisy started weighing on me. I had played six seasons to that point and had become a household name. Fantasy football coaches wanted me on their teams because of my consistent production and durability. I was buying into the hype about me. But the sinking realization that I was a hypocrite—that I wasn't living the way God wanted me to, despite my profession of faith—became too heavy of a burden to carry any longer.

I need to finally get serious about this, I told myself.

During times of worship, while the worship team sang songs from the platform, I started asking God to help me truly submit my entire life to Him. To submit to following His will instead of my own. To eliminate all the pride welling up in my heart.

I dedicated the rest of my life to following Jesus and was baptized at the conference as a public declaration of my decision.

For the first time, I knew the answer to the question I had first asked myself years ago when I wondered for what purpose God had gifted me with the ability to carry a football.

Through that ability, God had given me a platform from which I could seek out ways to share the gospel, not unlike I had after my first NFL game on *Sunday Night Football*, but also by modeling what it looks like to follow Jesus on a daily basis.

Unlike before, I would no longer settle for only going to chapels and Bible studies. I also had to read the Bible on my own, to ask God for discernment and revelation in reading His Word. When I started encountering God personally through Scripture, I could not hold my faith inside of me. In the gospel that bears his name, Luke writes that "[the] mouth speaks from the overflow of the heart."[3] The good news that Jesus died for my sins became so ingrained in me that I couldn't help but tell others that Jesus had done the same for them.

The moon is a dull rock, but it glows because it reflects the sun. When we commit—I mean *fully* commit—our lives to serving God, the "something different" people notice about us is our newfound ability to reflect the Son of God.

I wrote earlier that a graph of my faith journey would show a noticeable uptick when Danielle and I attended our first PAO conference. After our second conference, that graph would show a sharp increase that has continued to climb to this day.

---

[3] Luke 6:45.

17

CULTURE MATTERS

Before the league's first playoff game could be played, the front office signed Jay Cutler to a long contract extension, securing him as our quarterback. Changes were made in the defensive coaches, and the defense became a focal point of rebuilding, just as the offense had been the year before.

With most of our offensive pieces back, an improvement on defense in 2013 would surely have us back in the playoff picture, as well as contending for the division title.

Or so we thought.

We started the season with a close loss at home to Buffalo. We rebounded with back-to-back road wins against San Francisco and the New York Jets. Then we came back home to face the Packers, got bounced 38–17, and followed that with a loss at Carolina. Five games in, our offense was scoring four points fewer per game than the previous season, and defensive coordinators around the league seemed to have figured us out. Meanwhile, our defense still wasn't showing signs of being able to carry us like it had in the Lovie Smith era.

After the Carolina game, I learned a new word: *pectineus*. That's a muscle in the upper thigh that helps with hip adduction and flexion. Every time I tried to accelerate against the Panthers, my right hip killed me. As the game progressed, I lost my usual ability to accelerate.

Back in Chicago, I visited my physical therapist and described what I had felt during the game.

"Let me try some dry needling," he said.

Dry needling is also known as intramuscular stimulation, perhaps because that doesn't sound as frightening as dry needling. Thin, dry needles are poked through the skin into the muscle tissue. The needles are "dry" because nothing is injected into the body, like it would be with a vaccine, for example. With the needles, the therapist targets trigger points in the muscle, stimulating that area by causing the muscles to contract or twitch, which helps reduce the pain, decrease muscle tightness, and increase blood flow.

He had used dry needling on me before to help heal muscle injuries, and it had worked. But I still didn't like needles. This time, he said he wanted to stick needles into my groin muscle. I'd had doctors, trainers, and physical therapists stick needles all over my body. But until that moment, no one had stuck me in the groin. I started sweating.

The physical therapist said he had to find the trigger points. He could say that because the needles weren't being stuck into *his* groin. From my perspective, he was on a fishing expedition for these trigger points. Then he hit a spot that caused my right leg to jump.

"What's that?" I asked.

"That's your pectineus," he said.

I had never heard of it, so he explained what the pectineus does.

"This is uncomfortable," I told him.

"Let's see how it goes," he said.

He finished his work and sent me home. The next day, I practiced without a hint of pain. In one day, the dry needling had taken me from almost falling over in pain to there being no hint that I'd even had a problem in Sunday's game.

If only we could have dry needled our season.

Not Bought In

After the Carolina loss, we beat Atlanta 27–13. Then we lost three straight games, to Miami, New England, and Green Bay again. We lost to the Patriots 51–23 and to the Packers 55–14. We were 3–6 and spewing oil.

We bounced back to win our next two games, against Minnesota and Tampa Bay. But then, starting with a Thanksgiving Day loss at Detroit, we lost our final five games to end the season at 5–11. After finishing 10–6 the season Lovie Smith was fired, we had now gone a combined 13–19 in the two seasons after he left.

I topped 1,000 yards rushing for the third consecutive season, with 1,038. I also caught a whopping 102 passes—I was targeted 130 times—for 808 yards. The 102 receptions broke the nineteen-year-old NFL record for receptions in a season by a running back.

The day after our final game, general manager Phil Emery and coach Marc Trestman were both fired.

It's fair to say that the players were not surprised to see Trestman go after only two seasons. I don't think most of the guys ever bought in to his coaching style—especially on defense, because of how focused on offense the team became.

The Bears franchise has a long history of great defenses, dating to the Monsters of the Midway teams of the 1930s and 1940s. That nickname was resurrected for the Super Bowl champion 1985 Bears. With the city's winter weather and the Bears' outdoor stadium,

Chicago is a franchise that, with rare exceptions, will win because of its stout defense.

But Trestman wasn't fired because of the defense. I believe he lost his job because he lost control of the team's culture. Football is a tough sport that requires a tough mentality, and many players resented the soft vibes they picked up from Trestman. He was a good guy, and he was smart, but he was also rather soft-spoken. Someone who didn't know what Trestman did for a living might think he was a professor. Most teams reflect the personality of their head coach, and we just didn't have a good match with Trestman. Look at a coach like Dan Campbell of the Detroit Lions. He was a tough dude during his playing days—ten years in the league as a tight end—and he carried that mentality over to his coaching style. His players have picked up his toughness, and it shows in their success.

Culture Starts at the Top

In any profession, in any organization, culture is everything.

I've heard many definitions of culture, but I define it as the collective, consistent standard that is passed down from leadership.

Culture starts at the top, whether with the head coach or a CEO. *Starts* is the key word. The culture must be carried down the line, which requires buy-in at every level. Every person on the team or in the organization must accept the set standard.

In football, the quarterback and middle linebacker are often team captains because they are the players on each side of the ball who communicate the play calls and make adjustments at the line of scrimmage. Not every quarterback and middle linebacker possesses strong leadership skills, but they can lead by buying into the culture and the standards set by their coordinator or the head coach and playing in alignment with those standards. When they do, they carry the culture down to the next level.

Consistency is also crucial. If a team's culture is good one day and poor the next, it's never truly a good culture. Actually, if the target is moving every day, there probably isn't even a set culture. When that happens, each player sets his own standards. That leads to a mess on the field, in the locker room, and in the coaches' room.

Along with establishing the culture and standards, head coaches must also communicate vision. If a head coach walked into the first team meeting of training camp and said, "Our goal is to win the Super Bowl," guess what? Players on the thirty-one other teams in the league are hearing the same goal from their coaches. Everyone *wants* to win the championship, but players need to hear their coach's vision for *how* they will win the championship. Then the leaders on the team must model and echo that message every day, on the field and in the locker room.

Once a culture has been established and the expected standards are clear, new guys who join the team will either decide to get with the program or they'll stick out like a sore thumb. The question then becomes what happens with those guys who choose not to buy into the culture. A good culture will weed them out. I don't care how talented a player is; he must buy in to his team's culture or he's not worth having on the team.

The best teams have great leadership—on the coaching staff, among the players, and in the front office. Great leaders demand that pride and ego be checked at the door. They go about their business with a unity of goal, purpose, and standards. Those are the teams that are in the playoffs year after year. Then there are those teams that are in and out of the playoffs. Their lack of consistency keeps them from true excellence. And there is a group of teams that might sneak into the playoffs one year, but they're not considered playoff contenders every year.

The difference between those groups is their culture.

Where the culture is good, no player is bigger than the team, just like no employee is bigger than the company.

Because football is such a team sport, I had an appreciation for my role on the team as a running back. So many things had to go right for a play to be successful. I didn't snap the ball to myself or throw myself a pass. I didn't block for myself. As the running back, I was at the back of the line, and everything in front of me had to go right for me to make a play. When something went wrong, it was my job to find a way to compensate so our offensive unit could be successful. If someone missed a block, I had to make a defender miss. If a hole wasn't there, I had to make one or find one somewhere else.

That's why teamwork is so important, and teamwork flows out of the culture established at the top. When the culture is set, a team can develop an identity. Everyone wants to coach or play for a team that has an identity—that knows what it does best and can calmly go about its business even when it is behind and the clock is running out. But that is only possible after the hard work of building a culture has been completed.

Let's be honest about the NFL—it has become an entertainment business. Some players can make more money *because* they play football than they do by actually playing football. I'm all for players creating as much financial security as they can during the short time they have to play in the NFL. But not at the expense of a team's success. I played on teams that were talented across the board yet had terrible seasons. The reason often centered on culture. Players were allowed to pursue their own agendas and aspirations over team goals.

Just as it does in the corporate world, culture matters in the NFL.

18

A FEELING OF FINALITY

I entered the offseason ahead of the 2015 season all but certain it would be my last in a Bears uniform.

I was in the last year of my four-year contract and would turn thirty late in the upcoming season. The people who crunch data around the league set thirty as a benchmark for when a running back's performance begins to decline. Perhaps because I was a two-star recruit out of high school and didn't play my college ball in a major conference, I was accustomed to fighting against the opinions of those who liked to assign labels to players or stick them in groups that held them back in public perception.

With the firing of our general manager and head coach at the end of the previous season, we were already headed into an offseason of transition.

Ryan Pace was hired as our new general manager after working more than a decade in the Saints' front office. He was thirty-seven years old, which made him the league's youngest GM. Next, John Fox was hired as head coach. Fox had just left the Denver Broncos and was a veteran coach who had led two teams to the Super Bowl. His background was on defense. Fox brought Adam Gase with him from Denver to be our offensive coordinator, the role he'd held with the Broncos. Adam would be my fifth offensive coordinator with the Bears.

I hoped to play my entire career with the Bears and wanted to talk about a contract extension, but I set the date that I would report to training camp as a deadline to know whether this would be my last go-round with the Bears.

My agent expressed my desire to Ryan Pace, but I didn't expect the new GM to offer an extension before the deadline. I had been in the league long enough to know that keeping a soon-to-be-thirty running back going into his eighth season would not be a priority for a young general manager charged with rebuilding the roster to make the team competitive again. Brandon Marshall, who was thirty-one, had already been traded to the Jets, and my close friend Peanut Tillman was among a handful of players allowed to leave as free agents. Fourteen-year veteran center Roberto Garza was one of the players released.

Regardless of who was in charge, I had never felt fully welcomed by the Bears' front office. Signing my second contract had needlessly turned into an ordeal. The team kept bringing in running backs through free agency and had drafted a running back in the previous two drafts. I maintained my hold on the every-down role, but it always seemed as if the Bears were trying to find my replacement.

With all those considerations, I wasn't surprised, or even too disappointed, when there was no real attempt to sign me to an extension. At least I could start the season with a mindset of, "Let's go win some games and have some fun while we're winning." My desire to prove I could still be productive at a high level was no different than at the start of any of my previous seven seasons.

Based on our new coaching staff's commitment to the running game, I would have the opportunity to prove that. Every head coach will say that his team needs to run the ball to win games, but I believed that would be our identity on offense.

We opened the season by hosting the Packers. What better way to reassert ourselves as a playoff contender than by beating our rivals and NFC North favorites in the opener?

Once again, we had our chances yet came up short. With about six minutes left, we trailed by eight points and had the ball in Green Bay territory. But an interception killed the drive. The Packers turned that turnover into a touchdown, and though we responded with a touchdown of our own in the final minute, we couldn't recover our onside kick and lost 31–23. Still, our running game was encouraging. I rushed for 141 yards on twenty-four carries with a touchdown and caught five passes for 25 yards. I hadn't rushed for that many yards in a game since 2011.

I'm not a big believer in moral victories, but we came out of that game feeling positive about the offseason changes and about our potential to exceed the pundits' predictions that we would win only five or six games.

The next week's matchup, at home against the Arizona Cardinals, started as a back-and-forth affair—until midway through the second quarter. With us trailing 21–14 and looking to tie the game, the Cardinals scored on a pick-six, and Jay injured his hamstring on the play. We scored only field goals from that point on and lost 48–23.

In week three, we visited Seattle, the defending NFC champion. With Jay unable to play, we were shut out 26–0. Against a difficult schedule—all three of those opponents would win at least ten games that season—we were off to an 0–3 start.

I could see improvements not reflected in our record, and Coach

Fox brought an old-school mentality of toughness back to our team. But ever since the NFL had moved to its divisional alignment in 2002, no 0–3 team had turned its season around to make the playoffs. Speculation started among the media and fans as to whether, because of my contract status, the Bears should trade me in exchange for a draft pick to help the rebuild.

We won two of our next three games, though, and after the bye week we hosted Minnesota for a division game. Adrian Peterson was the Vikings' top running back. He had rushed for more than 1,000 yards in six of his first eight seasons to that point, including an incredible 2012 season in which he joined rarefied air among NFL running backs by topping the 2,000-yard mark.

During the previous summer, Kansas City running back Jamaal Charles had raised eyebrows around the league when he declared himself the LeBron James of NFL running backs. During the week before our game, Adrian was asked by the media about Jamaal's bold claim. He joked that must make him the Michael Jordan of backs. When a reporter asked Adrian to whom he would compare me, he said Steph Curry. "Mr. Dependable," he added. When the Chicago media asked for my reaction, I responded that I would accept that comparison, considering Curry's Golden State Warriors were reigning NBA champions.

I felt a little bit of extra motivation in a matchup like that one with Adrian. The motivation was not for comparing statistics after the game, but to run the ball well so our offense could control the clock and limit how much Adrian was on the field.

As it turned out, I didn't spend as much time on the field as I had planned. In the third quarter, I injured my right knee while being tackled after catching a screen pass. I limped off the field and to the bench, where the medical staff checked out my knee. After a few minutes, they took me to the locker room for a better evaluation. I was diagnosed with a sprained MCL. I would not need surgery, but I would have to miss a few games.

Farewell to Soldier Field?

I received a platelet-rich plasma injection to speed up the healing, but I still missed three games before returning for the Thanksgiving Day game at Green Bay. We were sitting at 4–6 on the season and had lost four consecutive games to the Packers. In fact, we had beaten them only twice in my career. The last time we had played at Lambeau Field, the Packers embarrassed us 55–14.

You hear TV announcers talk about professional teams out to get revenge against an opponent. Let me assure you, revenge games are real. I had received a taste of that in my NFL debut, hearing my teammates who had lost to the Colts in the Super Bowl talk all week about getting revenge in Indianapolis.

As I learned from my own experience, NFL players take note of everything—not only our opponents or certain games but even opposing players and specific plays. We watched a ton of film every week, and when we saw a player from the other team catch us off guard and deliver a big hit, we made mental notes for the next time we faced each other.

I didn't let the desire for revenge take away from my focus within the game, and I would never do anything dirty during a play or after the whistle had blown. But one of the beauties of football is the opportunity to legally even the score with someone.

When we played the Packers on Thanksgiving, I didn't have anything against an opposing player or any specific play. I was just tired of losing to the Packers—especially the aftertaste of the blowout we had suffered our last time at Lambeau. I couldn't remember how many Packers I had seen making the Lambeau Leap into the stands to celebrate a touchdown with their fans; but now we had a chance to pay them back in front of a nationwide football audience watching the holiday game.

On a chilly, rainy night, we got our revenge, defeating the Packers 17–13 and knocking them out of a tie for first place in the division. However, we lost our next three games before beating Tampa Bay, giving us a 6–9 mark going into the season's final game, at home against the Detroit Lions.

Leading up to the game, the Chicago media was interested in my thoughts about whether this would be my last game with the Bears. I told reporters I wasn't anxious and would be patient during the offseason, continuing to rehab and train while waiting to learn what decision Ryan Pace would make regarding my future with the team.

But I believed that would likely be my last game as a Bear.

We're not going to the playoffs, I thought. *So I want to put on a show. I need to at least score a touchdown.*

I'm not usually sentimental, but that game was an emotional one for me.

My game-day routine did not include going out to the field before our team's pregame warm-ups. Most players liked to go out onto the field and walk around, listen to music, throw a ball around, or whatever started getting them into their focus zone. I never did, choosing to stay inside the locker room to mentally prepare for the game.

For this game, I changed my routine, walking out onto the grass surface and soaking in the atmosphere. It was difficult to stop and appreciate moments in the NFL because events changed so quickly and careers were so transient. But on that day, I took time to stop and appreciate my eight years of calling Soldier Field home. I looked around at all the empty seats and reflected on all the games I had played with the seats filled with passionate Bears fans.

It took me until the fourth quarter, but I did score a touchdown that day. Fittingly for how I had committed myself to contribute in all phases of the offense, the score came on a pass instead of a run.

We had the ball on Detroit's 23. I ran a swing route to the left, and Jay's pass led me so that I caught the ball with my momentum going forward. I cut left around two defenders and started up the sideline. At the 10, I slowed up just a touch to allow time for a receiver to make his block; then I stepped inside of the block and ran through two attempted arm tackles and into the end zone.

Behind the end zone, I raised both hands to point heavenward and give the credit to God. When I turned back to face the field, my offensive teammates were running to congratulate me faster than usual after a touchdown. They knew how special a moment this was for me. They surrounded me, patting me on the helmet and embracing me. Jay stepped in to congratulate me. I tapped him on the helmet, and we put our arms around each other to head toward our sideline.

As I neared the sideline, Coach Fox stepped onto the field to embrace me. I tossed the ball to one of our equipment managers for safekeeping. Adam Gase was next to hug me. Based on the long cheers from Bears fans, I think the entire stadium felt the moment too.

We lost the game 24–20. We were driving for a go-ahead touchdown in the final four minutes, but our bid for a season-concluding victory ended with an interception deep in Detroit territory with two minutes to play.

After the final seconds ticked off the clock, I took a long, slow route off the field. I shook hands with the members of the chain crew and other sideline officials whom I had come to know through the years. I walked through the south end zone and along the stands to shake hands with and high-five fans as a way of saying thank you to them. Then I jogged across the field and into the tunnel on the north side of the stadium leading to the locker room.

I finished what was likely my last game as a Bear with 110 total yards, including 76 rushing on seventeen carries. For the season, I had rushed for 898 yards and added 389 yards receiving on forty-four catches. We finished the year with a 6–10 record.

I was prepared to be patient during the offseason to see if I could return to the only NFL team I had ever played for. I knew I would sign for less than fair market value to remain a Bear, and I expected the team to at least offer me a contract to open negotiations and see if we could work out a deal. If we couldn't, fine. At least we could say we tried.

The question, though, was, Did my team want me?

The Decision

Our season ended on January 3, and on February 12 Ryan Pace asked me to come to the Bears' facilities. Coach Fox was waiting with him in the general manager's office.

Their decision was delivered in a straightforward manner. I had played for the Bears a long time, I was told, and all I had done for the franchise was appreciated; but I would not be receiving an offer for another contract.

My response was something like, "Okay, thanks."

As simple as that, I knew my future, and it would not be in Chicago. When the NFL's new year started on March 9, I would officially become an unrestricted free agent able to sign with any NFL team.

I left the building and informed my agent.

At home, I posted the news on Instagram beneath a picture of me in my Bears uniform making a pregame entrance onto the field through smoke.

> Despite my wishes, my days as a member of the Chicago Bears have sadly come to an end. I was informed earlier this week from the GM that they will not be attempting to re-sign me in free agency. I will remain forever grateful

for my time spent in Chicago and being able to play for an organization with such a rich history. My only regret is not being able to win a Lombardi Trophy for the best fans in all of sports. I'm excited about the next chapter of my NFL career. But Chicago will always be home. God Bless and Bear Down!

I still loved football, but now I had to find a new place to play. That, too, is football, Son.

19

NEW YORK. NEW YORK?

The one team I wanted to play for no longer wanted me, so I became a free agent, able to sign with any team in the league.

The league calendar allowed for two days when teams could contact unrestricted free agents and enter into contract negotiations. But no deals could be signed until the free agency period opened on the afternoon of March 9.

Because of the knock on thirty-year-old running backs, I didn't anticipate a long list of teams would be pursuing me. Ultimately, five teams expressed some level of interest: the New York Jets, New England Patriots, Tampa Bay Buccaneers, Dallas Cowboys, and Green Bay Packers. Some media reports suggested the Packers had a serious interest in me. That was incorrect. They didn't offer me a contract, so I considered their interest pretty minor. But the thought of signing with the rival Packers presented an intriguing possibility.

The Jets were the first team to call. They said they considered me an every-down back and offered terms that I could accept: three years for $12 million, with $8 million guaranteed. I picked the Jets as my first team to visit and arrived at their facilities in Florham Park, New Jersey, ready to sign a contract. I went through a series of scans and X-rays, not as complex as at the Combine but enough to cover my most recent injuries.

The medical exams and waiting on the results seemed to be taking a long time. While I was waiting, Adisa called and asked for an update.

"I've already done the tour and all the other stuff," I told him. "Am I here to sign a deal or not?"

"Yeah," he said. "They're looking at your reports."

I expressed my frustration to Adisa. I was a running back with eight years in the league. They would not find a spring chicken on their X-rays and MRIs. The Jets knew my stats, had seen me on film, and had offered a contract. Something seemed off.

"What are we doing?" I asked Adisa.

"I've got the Patriots on the other line," he said. "They're interested right now. They said you can fly from LaGuardia and go visit them. But they don't have a contract on the table. They'd like you to go there and then negotiate a deal while you're there. But they aren't going to offer you one initially. What do you want to do?"

"I'm going to call you back in ten minutes," I replied.

I used those ten minutes to process what Adisa had just told me. The Patriots had Bill Belichick as their head coach and Tom Brady as their quarterback—two future Hall of Famers. They had just won their second Super Bowl in three years, and with all the dynasty talk surrounding their franchise, I didn't think I could have found a team that would offer me a better shot at playing in my first Super Bowl. LeGarrette Blount and James White were their top running backs, and LeGarrette was about my age. Brady liked to throw the ball to his running backs.

I called Adisa back. "Send me a car," I said.

On my ride to the airport, my phone rang. It was Mike Maccagnan, the Jets' general manager. I don't think he was at the team's facilities, because we were to the point that their contracts person could finish the process.

"I thought we had a deal," Mike said.

"Yeah, but I've been here for seven hours, and I've been sitting in the training room," I told him. "What are y'all doing? Y'all have been taking a long time, so I figured I'd go visit somebody else."

Mike didn't offer any excuses. He might not have known how long I had been waiting.

"We want you on the team," he said.

At that moment, a deep conviction struck me.

Am I a man of my word or not?

I had told the Jets I wanted to sign with them. From an integrity standpoint, how would it look if I allowed the Patriots to swoop in and steal me away? Before signing my second contract, I'd had a problem with the Bears saying publicly they would negotiate with me in good faith and then not doing so. The NFL is a business, but business is built on trust, and my parents had made sure the Forté name was associated with trust.

I asked the driver to take me back to the Jets' facilities, called Adisa, and told him I would not visit New England.

When I arrived back at the Jets' offices, I went in, signed my contract, and then headed back to the airport for a flight home to Chicago.

As strange as it sounded, I was now a New York Jet.

Making Adjustments

Danielle and I prayed and decided we wanted to keep our family together during the season, so she and the kids moved to New Jersey with me for the season. Because we would later return to our home in Chicago, it meant that our school-aged kids would have to split the school year between the two locations.

It's common for NFL families to remain at their permanent residence while the player moves to his team's city for the season. As a family guy, I don't know how those players can handle being away from their wives and kids for months at a time.

When I came off the field and walked through the door at home, I was no longer Matt Forté, football player. I was Dad. I had days off during the season when I could take the kids to school and pick them up in the afternoon. I didn't want to miss those moments, and I believed they needed their dad to spend that time with them in the car. Because our kids were young, they didn't have much school homework to help with, which meant I could hang out with them and just have fun.

We rented a home in New Jersey and had our vehicles shipped there. I was glad we didn't have to move everything we owned. Clothing was the most important thing we packed. I wear size 14 shoes, so my footwear took up a lot of room when we packed. I took advantage of my Nike contract to order shoes and have them shipped to our Jersey home.

My first experience with setting up a home in a new city made me feel for the journeyman players who move to a new team every year or two. For those whose football careers are lived on the edges of a roster, they are only one injury away from getting cut from the team so a new player can be brought in to replace the injured one. Players on the practice squad could be claimed by another team at any time. So, without much notice, they could be packing quickly to join their new team. It has to be rough living with that constant uncertainty.

My three-year contract with the Jets was essentially a two-year deal because of the guaranteed portion. Although we were living in two cities, Danielle and I had the luxury of knowing that, except for an unlikely in-season trade, I would be with the Jets for the entire season. And barring an injury, I would be back the following season as well.

From a football standpoint, I had to adjust to a new staff of coaches, including head coach Todd Bowles and offensive coordinator (number six!) Chan Gailey. I had new teammates, of course, though I reunited with Brandon Marshall, who had made his pitch for me to sign with the Jets after I knew the Bears would not try to keep me. I also had to adjust to new facilities, new team staff members who worked at the facilities, and even a new locker room—all important transitions in a sport where routine is crucial.

The most difficult change was figuring out how to bring my routines into a new environment. I'm an introvert, so I was not a guy who walked into a locker room and tried to liven it up. I needed time to make all the necessary adjustments.

The Jets had an amazing training facility compared to the Bears. They had excellent chefs and a great training room. Still, I had to get to know an entirely new training staff with the Jets. And I would have to rely on them, because I would no longer have access to the Chicago medical personnel and physical therapists with whom I had built up trust over my eight years there. I didn't know what to expect, but the Jets' trainers proved to be more concerned about the players' health than just getting them back on the field as quickly as possible.

Chan Gailey, the offensive coordinator, was a respected coach with head coaching experience in the NFL and at the major college level. Screen passes to the running backs were a prominent piece of his offense. Ryan Fitzpatrick had signed a one-year contract to remain the quarterback, so we had stability between the coordinator and the quarterback. The Jets had finished 10–6 in Todd's first season, but had missed the playoffs with a loss in their last game.

Though we played in the AFC East alongside New England, the Patriots would be without Tom Brady for the first four games because of a suspension for his role in Deflategate—a scandal surrounding the accusation that the Patriots had reduced the inflation on game balls in cold weather to give Brady a better grip on the ball. The football becomes very slick when it's cold outside, and the Patriots were looking for any kind of edge that would help them win games. Improving Brady's grip on a deflated ball while the opposing quarterback was throwing a fully inflated ball was one way to gain that edge. We faced a challenging schedule to start the regular season, but earning a postseason spot was a realistic expectation.

I was slowed during training camp by a hamstring tear I suffered while working out on my own before camp, but I was fully healed by the season opener at home against Cincinnati. We lost a heartbreaker, 23–22, on a field goal in the final minute. I accounted for 155 yards in my first game in green and white, rushing for 96 yards on twenty-two carries and catching five passes for 59 yards.

We had a quick turnaround for our next game, on Thursday night in Buffalo. We needed to recover a late onside kick by the Bills to win a high-scoring game, 37–31. I scored three touchdowns that night in addition to rushing for exactly 100 yards on thirty carries—the most carries in any game to that point in my career.

After those two games, we started seeing more defenders crowding the line of scrimmage as defensive coordinators focused on stopping our run game, forcing us to try to beat them by passing the ball. We lost our next four games, and my number of carries dropped with each one, from fifteen to fourteen to twelve to nine.

The New York media started asking whether I was wearing down. Age wasn't the problem. Instead, we had an age-old problem: NFL defenses eventually adjust to stop what's working for opposing offenses, and we could not adjust in response.

We ended our losing streak with a 24–16 defeat of the Baltimore Ravens, getting our running game back in form. I turned in my second thirty-carry, 100-yard performance of the season, with one touchdown. I also caught four passes for 54 yards and another score.

We won the next week, too, going on the road and beating Cleveland 31–28. I ran twenty-eight times for 82 yards and two touchdowns in that game. The next week, we lost 27–23 at Miami, but I ran for 92 yards and a touchdown on only twelve carries. I had another good game the next week in another loss, this one to the Los Angeles Rams, when I gained 98 yards on twenty carries.

The questions about my age and wearing down stopped.

I felt like the ol'—not *old*—Matt Forté from my Pro Bowl years with the Bears. Despite our rough four-game stretch when we struggled to run the ball effectively, I was fifth in the league in rushing yards, with 732, and tied for seventh with seven rushing touchdowns. I was on pace to rush for over 1,100 yards and could not recall the last time I felt as healthy as I did that deep into a season. With a 3–7 record, though, we were five losses behind the Patriots in the AFC East.

By week fourteen, we were 3–9 and riding another four-game losing streak going into our game at San Francisco. Our running game had fallen off again. Against the 49ers, I hyperextended my right knee in the first quarter. I felt clicking and popping in the knee and couldn't finish the game.

My left knee had been sore much of the season but had not caused any real problems. An MRI of my right knee revealed a meniscus tear, making me officially a game-time decision for our next game, against Miami. Bilal Powell started at running back, and I had only five touches. I injured a shoulder during the game, missed the next game, and then during the final week of the season, I underwent arthroscopic surgery to repair the meniscus tear.

We won our season finale against the Bills to finish with a disappointing 5–11 record. My final totals: 813 rushing yards with seven touchdowns, and thirty receptions for 263 yards and one score.

By the way, that was the season Belichick, Brady, and the Patriots overcame a 28–3 deficit to defeat the Atlanta Falcons 34–28 to win Super Bowl LI.

20

"IS IT WORTH IT?"

Let's be honest: Most people don't get excited to hear they must participate in a corporate team-building exercise. But before the 2017 season, we had one during OTAs with the Jets, and it made me wish we'd had one before my rookie season with the Bears.

A group of former military guys came in for three days of team-building and leadership talks. One thing they said that stuck with me was dispelling the myth that people rise to the occasion. I often hear that phrase while watching sports on TV, and I disagree with the idea every time.

The military guys told us that, in difficult circumstances, we always fall back on our training. They said that no one in the military became a better shooter because they were engaged in a battle. Their peak performance was determined not by their circumstances but by their training. If they depended on the battle to improve their shooting, they said, people would die.

Their talk hit me heavy. The football comparison was that no player would become a different level of player because of the context he was playing in. An athlete who doesn't prepare will be exposed, because when his team needs him to perform well, he will fall back on his training—that is, on his lack of preparation. A player would not outperform his preparation just because he was playing under the bright lights of *Monday Night Football*. How he played would be determined by how he had prepared for that moment in practice and by watching film.

The military guys also put us through a team-building exercise in water. They took us to a swimming pool and told us to jump in without further instructions. We did. Then they told us to pair up with a teammate and begin treading water. We were wearing thick hoodies, and we were told to take off our hoodies when a whistle blew, exchange hoodies with our partner, and put on the other guy's hoodie.

As you might imagine, the hoodies stuck to us in the water, making them difficult to remove. No set of teammates could complete the mission, so we had to keep treading water. I could see some of the guys getting scared as they began to tire. I'm a good swimmer, but I was getting a little shaky myself.

It was funny to watch guys try to figure out how to make the exchange. Some started quickly taking their hoodies off and throwing them to their partners. But in doing so, they were turning their hoodies inside out, which made putting on the hoodie even more difficult for their partner.

The point of the exercise was to teach us that helping someone else required making sacrifices of what was convenient for us.

Once I was safely out of the water, I loved what I had learned from our military friends.

Providing a Veteran's Voice

The failure of our 2016 team to make the playoffs led to a youth movement within the Jets to build for the future. Reporters speculated that our team would tank the season so we would wind up with a poor record and have a high draft pick for the following year. When asked about that as a possible strategy, I scoffed at the suggestion of doing anything at less than 100 percent effort. I responded to reporters' questions by saying that we were professional athletes and would give our best effort every week to win as many games as possible.

Offensive coordinator Chan Gailey retired during the offseason and was replaced by John Morton, the Saints' wide receivers coach. I hoped the change in coordinators would create more opportunities for Bilal Powell and me in the passing game. Under Chan, my pass-catching ability had been underutilized—my thirty catches and forty-three targets were by far my career lows. Chan had shifted me into more of a first- and second-down back and used Bilal on third down. Bilal was a good receiver out of the backfield. Especially considering how inexperienced we were at the receiver position going into 2017, I thought our offense would benefit from having Bilal and me on the field at the same time.

I didn't expect that would be the case, though, because John Morton said during the offseason that he believed in a running-back-by-committee approach instead of designating a feature back.

We also had a new quarterback join us who was not part of the youth movement. I was glad to be reunited with my buddy Josh McCown, who signed a one-year deal to be our starter at age thirty-eight. I was happy for Josh because this would be his fifteenth season in the league, and he hadn't received many opportunities to go into a season knowing he was "the guy" at quarterback. With our core of younger, inexperienced players, his strong leadership would be a plus on the field and in the locker room.

Early in training camp, I tweaked the opposite hamstring of the one I had hurt the year before. I had tried to rush my return from that hamstring injury and knew I would need to be patient during this camp. I didn't practice for more than three weeks to ensure I would be ready for the season opener.

For the first time in my career, I began thinking that retirement was nearing. This was my second hamstring injury in my two camps with the Jets. I had felt great during the season until the meniscus tear. The recovery time for injuries, though, seemed to be lengthening.

Bilal and I split carries in the first two games, both road losses. In the third game, at home against Miami, I injured the big toe on my left foot in the third quarter and left the game. X-rays were negative, and I was diagnosed with turf toe, a sprain of the main joint in the big toe. I had suffered the same injury on my other foot as a rookie. Turf toe is painful because of the pressure running backs place on their toes making cuts and even while blocking. The pain was more severe during my rookie year, and I didn't miss any games that season, so I was optimistic I would play in the next game. But I wound up missing two games, even with a cortisone injection in my big toe—one of the worst parts of the body for an injection.

Our team won both games by a field goal, and we were off to a surprising 3–2 start, tied with Buffalo and New England for first place in the AFC East. Next up: a home date against the defending Super Bowl champion Patriots.

I was able to practice that week and knew I would be able to play Sunday. Meanwhile, Bilal was dealing with a calf strain and would miss the game.

I shared time with Elijah McGuire against the Patriots, and we took a 14–0 lead in the second quarter. Then Tom Brady led the Patriots to two touchdowns before halftime to tie the score. In the fourth quarter, we trailed 24–17 when we got the ball at our own 27 with just under two minutes to play. We moved the ball into

Patriots territory with fifty-three seconds left, but we couldn't finish the drive and lost. New England did a good job of stuffing our running game, which was frustrating. I carried the ball nine times for 22 yards and contributed eight receptions for 59 yards. But despite all the preseason talk about how bad our inexperienced team would be, that was a game we should have won.

That loss started a three-game losing streak that included a particularly frustrating game against Atlanta. With rain expected for the game, we prepared a run-heavy game plan, and then abandoned it for reasons I didn't understand. Bilal had fourteen carries, and I had four, as our commitment to run the ball gave way to thirty-three pass attempts and only twenty-two rushes.

After we lost 25–20, I stood at my locker and answered reporters' questions, as usual. But what the media did with my interview provides an example of how the media can find a way to create controversy and clickbait when a team is losing. In response to one question, I said I thought we would've run the ball more than we threw it in a game with pouring rain. That would have been just about anybody's expectation, because when it rains like it did during that game, the ball is slippery and the risk for turnovers is high. One member of the New York media spun that simple comment into a story about a veteran challenging his offensive coordinator's play-calling.

The next day, I spoke with Todd and John to set the record straight, and we had a good conversation about ways we could win football games.

With a Thursday night game against Buffalo, we had a short practice week. And then guess what? We ran the ball forty-one times for 194 yards and won 34–21 to snap our losing streak. I had fourteen carries—my most to that point of the season—for a season-high 77 yards and two touchdowns. Bilal had 74 yards on nine carries. After the game, of course, the media wanted to hear my thoughts. I gave kudos to John for staying committed to the run game.

The break from the frustration didn't last long, though. We lost our next two games, won one, and then lost the final four games for another 5–11 finish.

The Ultimate Question

My right knee—the one I'd had offseason arthroscopic surgery on—swelled more than usual after the Buffalo game. Despite the extra time to recover following the Thursday game, I missed the next game and returned the following week. But after the week nine game against Buffalo, I felt like I played the rest of the season on one leg.

To rest my knee, I stopped practicing on Wednesdays and had limited participation the other days of the week. Now in my tenth year in the league, necessity required me to create a new method of getting ready for games with little more than mental preparation.

I had a bone bruise in my knee that didn't need surgery, just time to heal. We had the timeshare going in the backfield, and after a fifteen-carry, 58-yard game against Kansas City—our last victory—my carries dropped to six, seven, and eight, respectively, over the next three games. I tried to make an impact on the games wherever I could.

Every time I played, my knee swelled. "Ballooned up" is a more accurate description. My body's reaction to the bone bruise was to protect the joint with fluid. The day after a game, the fluid had to be drained from my knee. The needle to drain the fluid needed a good-sized opening, and the needles the team doctor used on me were about the width of a large straw. He inserted the needle into the quad above my knee and drained fluid into a 30cc tube. Every time he drained my knee, he filled three of those tubes. I watched my knee shrink as the fluid was removed.

My knee was drained every week for six weeks.

Toward the end of the season, the continuous swelling stiffened my knee to the point where I could barely flex it. My quad on that leg looked like it was withering away from atrophy.

In camp, the seeds of retirement had been planted in my mind. Now, as I went through the weekly draining just to be able to play, the *R* word worked its way into more conversations with Danielle. She saw me struggle with the physical pain and the mental toll of just getting ready to play and then not being able to produce near my normal level during games.

I was going through a difficult time.

"What percentage are you at?" became her question.

When my knee started flaring up, my answer was a 70 percent chance I would retire after the season. With a few weeks left in the season, my answer was up to 80 percent.

Each time she asked, she talked me through why I gave that answer. She was so incredibly sweet about it, because she didn't harp on me about needing to retire. Her concern for my future health was evident, but she was a supportive listener.

I didn't want to think about retiring. When I did, I tried to rationalize the possibility by telling myself that I'd had a lot of carries and catches over my eight years with the Bears that were catching up with me. Some years, I was on the field for 96 to 98 percent of our offensive snaps. In a perfect world, I would tell myself, that was too much to ask of a player. I wondered whether my career would have lasted longer if I had spent the bulk of it on a different team with a different culture, with perhaps not so much turnover among general managers and coaches—on a team where I wouldn't have needed to be the leading rusher and one of the top receivers.

But then the truth would snap me out of those thoughts. I had wanted to be an every-down back, and I relished staying on the field. I had nothing to regret about the way my career played out.

Besides, I was not fully convinced that I needed to retire. I had a year left on my contract with the Jets, and even though that year was not guaranteed and I didn't know if the Jets would want me back, I intended to fulfill the contract. I wouldn't need surgery like I had the year before, and maybe a good offseason of rest and rehab was all I needed to report back to training camp number eleven with 100 percent health.

Before the final game, the Jets placed me on injured reserve in a procedural move that opened a roster spot to bring a player from the practice squad to the active roster. My season ended with 381 rushing yards on 103 carries and two touchdowns, plus thirty-seven receptions for 293 yards and one score.

Would the 2017 season be my last?

I didn't know.

To help my knee heal, I chose to undergo stem cell therapy, which involved taking stem cells from the back of my hip and injecting them into my knee. I lay on a table, and even though I was numb from the waist down, I could feel pressure as the doctor drilled in with a needle to remove the stem cells.

I told Danielle I would allow time for the stem cell treatment to work, and after my knee had healed, I would give myself a physical test back home in Chicago before making a decision.

I expected the Jets to cut me. The third year of my contract was not guaranteed, and letting me go would make sense financially because of the salary cap. I could go through free agency again and probably catch on with a team as a third-down back to save wear and tear.

The past season had proved that I could still have an impact on games when I was healthy, so there was no question whether I could still play. The question was whether I could stay healthy. Playing while injured, I lost some of my elusiveness. That meant taking harder hits. More hard hits increased the risk of injury. And whether I played with the Jets or another team, it would mean another year of the kids splitting the school year between two cities.

The more I anticipated the decision ahead of me, as we headed back to Chicago for the offseason, I sensed that the ultimate question I would need to answer was, "Is it worth it to play another year?"

21

THE END OF A SEASON

"I'm going to the field."

Danielle knew what that meant.

"I'll see you when you get back," she said.

It was late February, less than two months after the 2017 season had ended. I grabbed a pair of cleats and drove to some soccer fields off of Chicago's Lake Shore Drive. I chose fields with an artificial surface like the Jets' home field because it is more difficult to make cuts on turf than on grass.

Music played in my SUV, but I wasn't listening to it. I was zoned out, focused only on one of the most significant workouts of my life.

I went alone. I needed to have this moment to myself. I didn't want anyone telling me how they thought I looked. I knew my body well. I knew how to listen to what it said.

I picked a field where I could have space and stretched and

warmed up my legs. Then, just like during those summer workouts back in Slidell when I simulated plays alone on our high school field, I called a play in my head, lined up in the backfield, took a pretend handoff from a quarterback, made a cut, and accelerated through a crease in the offensive line. I returned to my spot and repeated the play a second time.

My body quickly returned its verdict.

When I made a cut, my knee hurt. Twenty-five seasons of football, 189 games in college and the NFL, had worn down the cartilage in my knee. Like driving a car that needs new brake pads, I could feel grinding in my knee.

On the way home, I opened the sunroof in my SUV and rolled down my windows. No music this time. The only sound was the wind. I felt peace as I drove. And a sense of joy.

I knew I could play another year. I still had juice in my legs, and I could tough out the knee pain again if necessary. Danielle was willing to put the kids in a new school in a new city one more time. But to answer the question, playing another season would not have been worth it.

The truth was that I had more left in the tank physically than I did in my heart for the game. I still loved football, but the relationship had changed. I didn't know how much longer I wanted to be in pain every day during a season. I had never suffered a concussion, and I didn't want to take any more chances with that.

For ten seasons, it didn't matter if I'd had a Pro Bowl season, a bad season, or anything in between—I had never had the luxury of sitting back and reflecting on what the Lord had allowed me to accomplish on the field. The NFL is tough. Even after a great season, I could not afford to have any drop-off the next year, or I would hear about how I was wearing down. My replacement always seemed to be trying to take my job from me. There was no time to sit and enjoy the successes. But as I neared home, I felt gratified. I had accomplished what

God had called me to do as a football player. I could leave football, satisfied and comfortable because football wasn't retiring me.

I walked in our back door. Danielle had heard the garage door and met me in the entryway.

We looked each other in the eye. I shook my head no.

She reached out to hug me, and we held a long embrace.

When we stepped back, she asked how I felt about my decision.

"I'm good," I told her.

I felt a sense of relief for Danielle.

She had watched me in pain at home. Many times, she had woken up in the middle of the night and watched me limp from our bed to the restroom. She had looked over to my side of the bed and seen blood on the sheets from the cuts on my legs and arms.

She had learned to become a combination physical therapist/counselor at home, although she was trained for neither. She spent many nights digging her elbows into my hamstrings, trying to drive out the tightness. She had learned how to stretch me out. She had listened to me and counseled me after losses and seasons that ended without making the playoffs and during aggravating contract negotiations.

But those days were behind us now. Finally, they were behind her.

That night, I called my parents, and my mom answered. She was used to Danielle calling to talk to them and me jumping in on their conversations. I told Mom I had some news for them, and she called my dad over to the phone.

"I'm retiring from football," I told them.

I didn't hear any surprise in their voices. They just wanted to know how I felt.

"Good," I assured them.

"You know," my dad said, "ten years is a long time for a running back. You beat the odds. You've done well."

My parents had affirmed me throughout my career, from youth

sports on up. I had always felt their support. "You've done well" was all I needed to hear from them.

A Time for Reflection and Appreciation

I chose a unique platform to announce my retirement: Sports Spectrum, a Christian sports media podcast, hosted by my friend Jason Romano. He had interviewed me a few times before, and I liked the opportunity Sports Spectrum provided athletes and coaches to share their faith with sports fans, knowing that their faith stories would be told in full without being edited down or left out completely.

My faith trajectory had been on an incline, starting with the first time Danielle and I attended a Pro Athletes Outreach conference. The upward slope increased even more after the second conference. When I look back at my time in the NFL, it's interesting that my football trajectory seemed to run opposite of my faith trajectory. Down seasons on the field often drove me into a closer relationship with the Lord. Over my final two seasons with the Jets, I experienced a noticeable growth in spiritual maturity.

When Jason asked toward the end of my retirement interview what was next, I said that when people wanted me to reflect on my NFL career, I would be able to share the gospel with them by explaining how good God had been to me throughout my career.

Once the news went public, there seemed only one fitting way to officially retire.

The NFL, like other professional leagues, allows a player to sign a ceremonial one-day contract with a team so he can retire as a member of a team that was special to him earlier in his career. I appreciated the opportunity the Jets gave me to play two seasons with them. My experience with them was first-rate. But my heart belonged to the team that took a chance on me by drafting me in the second round. Devin Hester, my good friend and former teammate, had announced his retirement near the end of the 2017 season. Though he had played for three other teams after leaving Chicago, he was most associated with the Bears and—like me—wanted to retire as a Bear.

On April 23, 2018, Devin and I held a retirement ceremony together at Halas Hall, where we signed one-day contracts with the Bears and then officially retired. I had spent eight years at Halas Hall. Driving through the entry gate brought a sense of nostalgia. So did walking into the facility wearing a suit and tie to look professional for my last day with the Bears—just as I had on my *first* day.

Holding a retirement ceremony provided special moments for my family, as well. I hadn't felt a need for closure on my career or with the Bears, but I thought my family might because they had lived the journey with me. I had never truly celebrated my successful seasons. But now we could, together, celebrate a successful career.

Former teammates and a few current Bears players showed up to honor Devin and me, which made the day even more memorable.

By then, I'd had some time to reflect on my career. I was asked numerous times if I had been tempted to play one more season to achieve a significant milestone—10,000 career rushing yards—which I needed only 204 yards to reach. No, I was not tempted. Less frequently talked about was another milestone: 15,000 career yards from scrimmage. I was only 534 yards short of that mark. Running backs are usually measured by their rushing yards, but total yards was always a telling statistic for me because it included receiving yards. Still, the answer was no. I didn't *need* to reach any statistical milestones.

I understood why reporters and fans asked that question. I realized that 10,000 yards sounds different than 9,800. But what difference would 200 more yards really make? Adding 200 yards to my rushing total over a ten-year career would not have meant anything more to me than what I had already accomplished on the field.

Retiring as a Bear brought back to the forefront the number of categories in which I ranked only behind the great one, Walter Payton, in the franchise's all-time stats. Having my name mentioned with Payton's started when I was a rookie, and back then, I would always say it was way too early in my career for those comparisons. At the end of my career, it was still not even close. I rushed for 8,602 yards as a Bear. Payton rushed for almost twice as many—16,726. Obviously, my career didn't warrant any level of comparison to his. Nonetheless, as far as leaving a legacy goes, having my name mentioned in the same conversation as Payton's was gratifying. He was the best running back to play in the NFL. I am quite content to be considered one of the best backs to play in Chicago.

Over the years, Chicago became a special place for me. I still live there, and my parents left Louisiana to live there too. Chicago sports fans have a deep passion for the Bears. While I was still playing there, fans I would see around the city would thank me for what I was doing with the Bears. But after I announced my retirement, I think my connection with the fans grew even stronger.

We had endured some rough years with our offense, and the fans justifiably felt frustrated. But Chicago is a blue-collar city, and once my playing days were over, the fans became more vocal about expressing their appreciation for my hard work and playing through pain regardless of what type of season we were having.

I felt few regrets when I decided to retire, but none was larger than not winning a Super Bowl for Chicago. Bears fans have gone far too long without one, and they deserve another. My teams could not end the long wait, but I hope a Bears team will soon bring the Lombardi Trophy back to our city.

22

STILL IN THE GAME

I retired at age thirty-two. I have seen firsthand—as a player and in retirement—how difficult the transition from professional athlete to former pro athlete can be.

For my transition, I went back to my dad's example of being prepared for life after football. He'd had his collegiate playing career before I was born, so I only saw him working hard for Shell to support his family. But he always emphasized the importance of getting an education. I remembered the advice he gave me over the years: "I played football growing up and in college. You don't know what's going to happen. Don't put all your eggs in one basket."

My association with Pro Athletes Outreach had reoriented me toward finding the purpose of my platform in the NFL and how I would extend those opportunities beyond my playing career. In the process, I began to recognize that stats, highlights, and accolades had a short shelf life. What would matter in the long run was how I lived out my faith.

The latter half of my career was a time of learning how to reflect the light of God that shines on me, so that when people requested an autograph or asked questions about playing in the NFL, I could point them toward God as well. None of that would end with my retirement from football.

The question I'm asked most often today is, What do you do now? The specific answer has changed a few times, but in a broad sense, I have dedicated my post-football work to ministry.

Still, the transition out of football necessitated adjustments that have not always been easy.

For one, I had to find a new routine. There were days, especially early after my decision to retire, when I didn't know what to do with my time. I realized how many of my life's routines were built around football. Our games were scheduled for us, our practices were scheduled for us, our meetings were scheduled for us, and our off-season OTAs and camps were scheduled for us. Now, my schedule was entirely up to me.

I felt the temptation to jump right into my next job, whatever that might be. But during my prayer time, I sensed the Lord telling me to take time to enjoy my family. My new routine included more of taking the kids to school, picking them up afterward, and doing homework with them. I wanted to continue working out, and I found that doing it early in the day brought mental clarity that helped me for the rest of the day.

I stayed connected to football by taking a job with a Chicago TV station as an in-studio analyst on the day of Bears games. I had always been interested in broadcasting, so that was a fun opportunity that required little time commitment.

An unexpected opportunity to leverage my platform came when

Danielle and I were introduced to a ministry called Biblica that translates and shares the Bible so people in the far corners of the world can have access to and engage with Scripture.

Rashied Davis, a former Bears teammate, introduced Danielle and me to Biblica's work when he asked me to record a simple testimony video about the importance of God's Word. Danielle befriended a woman who worked at Biblica and learned from her about an upcoming missions trip to India. Danielle had gone on a missions trip to the Dominican Republic during high school, and she wanted both of us to go on the India trip. Similar to when Josh McCown first invited me to a Pro Athletes Outreach conference, I wasn't a big fan of the idea. I hadn't been retired long and was still trying to keep my schedule light. And I wasn't too interested in flying eighteen hours to India. But I went. I was dragging my feet, but I went.

The trip changed many of my perspectives. I gained a whole new sense of love for the people of other nations. I realized how privileged we are in the United States. I watched in awe as kids living in extreme poverty played with such joy on their faces. I learned what a "heart language" is—people's mother tongue, or native language, that they understand best—and that tens of millions of people around the world don't have even a single verse of God's Word in their heart language. At best, they have Scripture in only a trade or broader language. I couldn't help but think of all the different translations and versions of the Bible I had access to back home, and yet so many people in the world don't have access to one. I heard stories of places that had been waiting for a hundred years or more to have an accurate Bible they could understand.

When I saw people's lives transformed by their first encounter with God's Word in their native language, I found Kingdom work I wanted to get involved in. After we returned home, Danielle and I started working with Biblica as global advocates. During our time with Biblica, we met a man who risked his life to smuggle Bibles into countries where it was forbidden. Another man told us how he hid Bibles at the bottom of crates containing jars of honey to smuggle them into closed countries. We laughed because Psalm 119:103 says of God's Word, "How sweet your word is to my taste—sweeter than honey in my mouth." We attended ceremonies in countries where people groups had just received either a complete Bible or portions of Scripture in their language. People would cry, laugh, and shout in celebration at finally having access to the life-giving power of Scripture.

Observing those Bible launches and being around people who risked persecution—even to the point of death—so that others could have access to the Bible, removed the word *routine* from how I lived out my faith. Having a Bible in my home or attending church never cost me anything. But my visits to India and other countries opened my eyes to see what it cost me *not* to treasure Scripture.

I began consistently opening up God's Word. I read through the entire Bible for the first time. I studied commentaries that helped me dig deeper into Scripture and gain a fuller understanding of what I believed.

Earlier, I quoted one of my favorite verses, Matthew 6:33: "Seek first the kingdom of God and his righteousness, and all these things will be provided for you." My spiritual maturity grew as I learned to seek God first. I experienced an intimacy with Him that I had never known. After years of having a transactional relationship with God, I discovered what it meant to be in a genuine relationship with Him.

Discovering True Love and Forgiveness

My spiritual growth led me back to PAO—but this time to walk alongside athletes on their spiritual journeys.

The sad truth is that a majority of professional athletes wind up filing for bankruptcy or divorce. My purpose became to do what I could to help those still in the season of their playing careers prepare for the season to follow—which most are not prepared for.

I wanted to tell them about the temptations I had faced so that—even if they hadn't faced them yet—they would be prepared to respond well. I wanted to show them how they could be advocates for Christ *now*. I wanted them to see what it looks like when God is no longer an accessory to their lives but the center of their lives.

So, Danielle and I joined PAO's staff.

On the financial side, I talk to athletes about saving money for the rest of their lives instead of spending it all. The temptation is to live a fancy lifestyle because they're suddenly making more money than they've ever seen. But most NFL contracts are not guaranteed, so that income can get cut off in a hurry. Also, an athlete's money doesn't last as long as you might expect. Taxes on athletes' salaries are high, there are agent and management fees, and we often pay people to help us with our health and nutrition so we can stay competitive in our sport. As someone once told me, "Making a lot of money costs a lot of money." That's the truth.

I was smart with my money during my playing days, and as I matured spiritually early in my retirement, I noticed a lack of nervousness or anxiety about finances. In Philippians 4:19, Paul writes, "My God will supply all your needs according to his riches in glory in Christ Jesus." I have found that to be true. But as I read stories about athletes filing for bankruptcy, my heart was moved to find a platform that would allow me to talk with current athletes before it was too late for them.

I mentioned that Danielle is also on staff at PAO. As a couple, our focus is on athletes' marriages. Our passion in that area comes from our own difficult experiences that easily could have ended our relationship. She and I pray that our story of forgiveness, redemption, and unconditional love will bring hope to other athletes and their marriages.

Power of Presence

In retirement, I can dedicate more time to the What's Your Forté Foundation. During my playing days, my availability was limited to mostly summer programs.

We have an executive director who has helped us organize the foundation better, allowing us to more effectively collaborate with organizations and individuals committed to similar causes in Chicago.

These collaborations led us to create a career camp in partnership with some of the city's top companies. The camp teaches young people and adults how to attain jobs and succeed in life. The Your Forté, Our Finance program creates business opportunities for young African American entrepreneurs while investing in marginalized and underinvested communities. Reach4Life is an outreach and discipleship program for at-risk teens and young adults. The forty-week program consists of classes focused on four topics we believe are life-changing: believing, growing, living, and changing. Through the classes, we teach young people coping skills for facing life's challenges and becoming agents for change in their families and communities.

I wanted the foundation to focus on being practical to change life trajectories. A real estate expert has taught residents in underprivileged communities how to purchase a two-flat and rent out one of the units to pay for the whole building, which allows them to not spend their work income on housing. A construction company has hired people through our foundation for well-paying jobs. We have worked with banks to provide small-business loans that allowed entrepreneurs to own their place of business instead of spending money on rent and leases. We have introduced youth to career options to become culinary professionals and pilots and to work in media.

How does all that relate to my original purpose of gun violence prevention?

As I started working with the youth in Chicago, I met kids who told me it was easier to get a gun than a book. When I encouraged them to put down their guns, they would ask what I was going to give them to pick up instead. I quickly learned that a message of "put down your guns and stay in school" offered no value to kids. They wanted to know what would put food on their table for their next meal. It wasn't that these kids weren't looking for a better way to live; they simply lacked access to people who could show them the way to a better life.

The idea of access and exposure became important to me so we could introduce these young people to opportunities they didn't know existed. One example was a visit our foundation arranged to a local television news station. There, the kids could see potential careers beyond just those they could see in front of the cameras. They discovered they could become producers, directors, camera operators, writers, and hair and makeup artists.

I cannot describe the joy of seeing their eyes opened to previously unknown opportunities. We never know what access can do to inspire people to dream and discover careers that align with their long-held passions.

At first, I thought leveraging my association with the Bears would make running the foundation easy. It turned out to be hard work and time-consuming, which is why we have been able to expand our offerings since I retired. I have learned the importance of not just attaching my name to a good cause but also being part of the work.

I still carry a lesson learned from a kid in my foundation's early days that has shaped how we run What's Your Forté.

Former Chicago Bull Joakim Noah had a foundation called Noah's Arc that fought gun violence through basketball and art. Joakim would go into Chicago's toughest neighborhoods to hang out with the kids. I decided that to have an impact on young people, I needed to understand their world. I knew where I wanted to lead them to, but I didn't know where I needed to lead them from.

I chose the Englewood neighborhood and started going there on Saturday mornings to play flag football in an open field behind a recreational center. I told the kids to put out the word that Matt Forté would be there on Saturdays to play football with them.

Each week, I planned a topic I wanted to talk to the kids about, and we took a break from playing flag football so I could give them life lessons I didn't think they were hearing at school or home.

My third week in Englewood, a boy walked up to me and said, "Man, you keep coming back."

"Of course I'm going to come back," I said. "I told you I'd be here."

"That's cool," he said. "Most of the time, people just come once, and they come to do one thing for the cameras. They come here, take pictures, and leave. You don't have any cameras. You're just out here playing."

"We're all human beings," I told him. "Just because I do something different than people you know, and just because I get to be on TV playing football, doesn't mean I'm better than you. You have a special gift and talent that God has placed in you, and He has a purpose for your life."

I learned how much the kids valued the presence of positive adult influences. They responded to my consistently being in their neighborhood. Then they started trusting me enough to ask questions they had about life. That was when the real impact began.

Living in Purpose

As the foundation grew, my retirement allowed me to increase my presence and provide more adults who could maintain a positive presence in those neighborhoods. Faith is an essential element of our foundation. Though we are not a faith-based foundation, per se, I and other Christians associated with our foundation never shy away from talking about Jesus.

The reward is seeing lives changed.

One example is the barbershop owner who was in danger of losing his business during COVID. Many Black-owned businesses in the neighborhoods where our foundation works struggled to stay afloat during the pandemic. We partnered with a bank that provided small-business loans and help to entrepreneurs. I came to know one barbershop owner who contacted that bank. He had been leasing his place of business. As part of the process of obtaining a loan, he received business training that educated him on how to purchase the location instead of renting. As the shop owner, he could make more income by not paying rent. He paid off the loan, and now he and the other barbers working in his shop have higher incomes, which they use to better provide for their families and put money back into their community.

Another success story is about a man who dreamed of opening a gym in his South Side neighborhood. The man had the location picked out but didn't know how to make his dream come true. Our foundation assisted him with acquiring a small-business loan to purchase equipment and helped him prepare to open the gym. He brought in trainers to hold classes and promote working out for living healthier lifestyles. His gym is making a difference for the people in his neighborhood.

And then there are stories like Kola's.

Kola was ten or eleven when I started my flag football Saturdays in Englewood. After I retired, Kola was one of the kids I saw weekly for a while. I gave him my phone number and told him to keep in touch. Kola texted me years later to let me know he was about to graduate from high school. In the neighborhoods where our foundation works, graduating high school is a big deal. Part of our focus is trying to help kids who tell us they don't think they will live long enough to finish high school. Recognizing the significance of his accomplishment, I texted Kola back to congratulate him and tell him how proud I was of him.

In the conversation that followed, I asked Kola if he attended church, and he told me he attended the church he grew up in. I told him to let me know if he ever wanted to visit the church my family attends. Charlie Dates is our church's pastor. I met Charlie through PAO, and he became one of my best friends. Charlie counseled me numerous times on the phone as I contemplated retiring and then discipled me through my transition out of football. One thing I liked about Charlie was that, instead of asking me how I was doing, he would ask, "How is your *soul* doing?"

Charlie cares deeply for people, and our church does a lot for the community, including providing food and housing for the underprivileged.

Kola visited us one Sunday, came back again, and kept coming back until he joined the church. Then he started bringing family members with him, and then friends. The section we sat in with Kola began filling up on Sundays with people new to our church.

Kola is now a student at DePaul University, studying to become a sports agent. My agent, Adisa, is mentoring Kola to guide him on the path to becoming a sports agent after college.

Two things come to mind when I reflect on Kola's story.

First, the multiplying power of one invitation. I invited Kola to visit church with us, and he accepted. Josh McCown invited Danielle and me to attend a PAO conference, and we accepted. Josh's invitation had a ripple effect—from me to Kola to many of Kola's friends, who began a personal relationship with Jesus Christ because Kola invited them to church.

When we extend an invitation to someone, we don't know whether it's the first one they've received or the third or fourth—which might be the confirmation they need to finally accept. I look at invitations as seeds. In our spiritual battle, the enemy knows he cannot stop God's work, but he can cause us to doubt ourselves so that we don't plant the seeds. I no longer concern myself with whether a person will respond to an invitation, reject me, or get mad at me. I will still plant that seed so God can do His work in His perfect timing.

Second, Kola's story reminds me that God gave me the gift of running with a football for a purpose, and even though my days on the football field are behind me, God's purpose remains alive in me. I don't know if I could imagine two more polar-opposite environments than a room full of professional athletes and a neighborhood in south or west Chicago. But there is one stunning similarity: In both environments, people are seeking their God-given purpose. In this season of life, my purpose is to help them figure that out and find the pathway to fulfilling their purpose.

I am still in the game—the most important game there is—playing every down to point people to Christ.

Over the course of my college and NFL career, I played on teams that lost more games than we won. But in this game, victory is assured. As the apostle John writes near the end of the Bible, "Everyone who has been born of God conquers the world. This is the victory that has conquered the world: our faith."[4]

This book has an ultimate purpose as well, and it is to ask you this question: If you have not accepted Jesus Christ as your Lord and Savior, will you do so today?

I would be honored to be your teammate!

---

[4] 1 John 5:4.

Epilogue

Thank you for reading this book. In closing, I want to speak directly to collegiate and professional athletes. Can we consider this a locker room talk from a former athlete to those of you still in the arena of competition?

Adam Gase became the offensive coordinator for my last season with the Bears, in 2015. I had played seven years in the league, and by that point I assumed my play spoke for itself. I believed in leading by example. (The military guys who visited when I was with the Jets two years later convinced me this was wrong thinking.)

At the end of training camp, as final cuts were being made to set our fifty-three-man roster for the regular season, Adam asked me to speak to a gathering of offensive players who had made the cut.

My first thought was, *You want me to speak in front of the guys?*

Adam's request was one typically made of the starting quarterback. In 2015, that would have been Jay Cutler. I accepted hesitantly because my style was to model hard work on the practice field. If I saw somebody slacking off, I would say, "Hey, man, we gotta step it up. We don't do it like that here"—and then get right back into the huddle for the next play.

As I planned what to say, I wanted to be authentic and both encourage and challenge my teammates.

I remember acknowledging the reality that we had yet another offense to install under a new offensive coordinator. We also had a new head coach and a new general manager.

"There are probably a lot of people on other teams looking at the schedule and writing a *W* next to the Bears game," I said. "But as I look at the eyes of the guys in this room, if I could say something to those other teams, I would tell them they'd better write those *W*'s in pencil, because when they play us, we're going to write an *L* for them in ink."

My teammates perked up!

I also recounted to them the scene from *Forrest Gump* when Forrest was in the military, and he and Bubba were sitting next to each other in a heavy rain. Bubba told Forrest that he would lean his back against Forrest's so neither one would have to sleep with his head in the mud. Then Bubba delivered that memorable line: "You know why we a good partnership, Forrest? Cuz we be watching out for one another. Like brothers and stuff."

The offensive players who made the fifty-three-man roster, I told my teammates, needed to be back-to-back and looking out for each other. "I'm talking about sacrifice," I continued, "where just because I'm not getting the ball doesn't mean I take a play off. Or just because I'm on the back side of the play doesn't mean I slack off and get some rest. I want to challenge you guys to go 100 percent all the time. I don't care if the world considers you a superstar or a seat-filler. When you walk into this facility, the ground is level. As a matter of fact, the lower you are, the greater you'll be!"

A teammate asked, "What do you mean by that, the lower I am, the greater I'll be?"

I explained that true greatness comes only by serving, and everyone has the ability to serve. "The more we serve each other as teammates," I continued, "the better we'll be as a whole organization."

My talk ran counter to the typical selfishness of the NFL and professional sports in general. The common thought for athletes is to get everything they can while they still can, to use up the game before it uses them up. But one way or another, the game always takes its dividends.

Our offensive players bought in to what I was saying because they knew I spoke the truth—the truth about football and about life. I spoke to the heart instead of the ear.

From that day on, I thought more critically about what to say to my teammates and how to focus on what was really important so we wouldn't gloss over something that could come back to haunt us. A common saying used by teams or players who have gotten too comfortable with losing is "We'll get it next time." But that attitude was no longer acceptable to me. Real leadership makes *urgency* a priority so that little problems don't become big problems later. I became a player who always emphasized the importance of preparing to win *today*, not waiting for tomorrow. Success requires a sense of urgency.

I don't know if Adam saw something in me as a person or my status as a seven-year veteran that I didn't see in myself, but he removed my contentment to lead by example. We think of coaches as *calling out* their players when they make mistakes. That day, Adam called me *up* as a leader. And now I want to do the same for you. Just as when I was addressing my Bears teammates, I aim to be authentic while encouraging and challenging you.

The most important person you will ever lead is yourself. The most challenging person to lead is yourself. You cannot lead others well if you do not first lead yourself well.

When it comes to leadership, it's impossible to give someone what you do not possess. You cannot pass down wisdom that must be searched for, strived for, and learned through experience. You cannot pass on character traits like grit, determination, loyalty, integrity, and toughness without the discipline to live out those traits yourself. If you are not disciplining yourself and leading yourself that way first, your leadership will hit its cap far too soon. At some point, you will be revealed as a hypocrite for calling others to a higher standard if you don't meet that standard yourself.

As a collegiate or professional athlete, you know how few of your peers have reached the level you have. You are in a rare category of athletes. God has blessed you to compete at your level. But He did not bless you only for yourself. What is your purpose as an athlete? You should ask yourself that question day and night until it is clear what purpose God created you for. Here's a hint: If your answer is not about you, you're on the right track! If your answer begins with "So I . . . ," back up and start over.

I am passionate about this topic because of how long I sought to find my purpose in football. Throughout my playing days, I knew that football was not my be-all and end-all. But I did not quite understand how I could be significant rather than merely successful.

I am passionate because I want *you* to get it right at a younger age than I did.

We live in a culture that is all about me, me, me; and college and pro sports magnify that idea even further. The more attention you receive because of your athletic ability, the easier it becomes to believe that everything truly is all about you.

The ear tests words just as the mouth tastes food. So I want you to have the wisdom from God to put His filters over your ears so that your heart and mind do not feast on the junk food of people always praising you. God designed you to reflect His glory, not to accept it as if you were Him and essentially play God. Just because something tastes good (or sounds good) doesn't mean it's good for you. You can feed on snacks and junk food all you want because they taste good, but in the end, you'll be malnourished and full of junk, with no appetite for what your body and soul really need. But God can give you a new appetite and desire for His purpose. You have seen that in my story.

God has given you the platform you have now for you to use *now*. If you understand that everything is about His glory and not yours, you will have a shield against the "me" temptations and be available for God to utilize while you're at your most influential. Let me assure you, when your playing days are over, your influence will diminish. Often rapidly. I don't care if you're Tom Brady or Drew Brees. As soon as they retired, everyone was talking about Patrick Mahomes and Lamar Jackson. And when Mahomes and Jackson retire, they'll focus on the next generation of quarterbacks. That cycle will continue.

Don't wait to use your influence for God. Your usefulness doesn't have to be delayed or diminished because of your youthfulness. God has placed you where you are *now*, so allow Him to use you now. You are not the first person to walk this pathway in your sport, and you will not be the last. Show others coming up behind you how God is working in your life on the path you are still walking. Strive to be *significant* more than you desire to be successful.

I would fail you if I encouraged you—challenged you—to play your sport and live your life with purpose without also including *how* to find your purpose. I know from experience that finding your purpose can be a struggle. But it doesn't have to be.

First, understand that God created you for a purpose beyond your sport. That is great news because your playing days will end. I retired at thirty-two, and very few players play even as long as I did. Your purpose will remain with you when your playing career ends. But it starts by acknowledging that God has a purpose for you that is far bigger than you.

To find that purpose, you need an ear attentive to what God tells you.

We too often make the mistake of sitting down and saying, "All right, God. Tell me my purpose." I believe that God hits moving targets. My experience is that when I start taking action, God makes

His path for me clear. I like the phrase *step of faith*. When we take a step of faith, believing that God will reveal His path to us, He does. He isn't keeping a secret from us. He doesn't create an individual plan for each of us and then prevent us from knowing that plan.

Second, God gives us an appetite for our purpose. Our purpose and our passions align. God doesn't call us to do something we hate. He can call us to something that is uncomfortable, or in an area where we lack confidence; but He equips us to do what He calls us to do. He wants us to succeed in His plan. He is *for* us. He is for *you.*

Our passions will help us through the days when our emotions cast doubts or fears. Emotions are fickle, but God calls us to what we are passionate about so our path will be one we will not want to turn away from. As our appetite is continually satisfied, we are nourished to carry on with our purpose. In Ecclesiastes 3:11, Solomon writes that God placed eternity in the human heart. God's work is eternal work. When you are working according to your God-given purpose, you feel fulfilled.

Gideon is one of my favorite Bible characters. His story is told in the Old Testament, in Judges 6–8.

Gideon is considered the greatest judge in Israel during Bible times. But the picture his story paints is initially one of a timid man, called by God to deliver Israel from its enemies. Gideon had many doubts about himself, and he kept asking for signs that God was indeed calling him to lead Israel to military victory. As Gideon persisted in expressing his doubts, God sent an angel to him with a message. At the time, Gideon was threshing wheat while hiding in a winepress so the Midianites wouldn't see him and come steal the wheat. And this was the angel's message: "The Lord is with you, *valiant warrior*."[5]

Valiant warrior?

---

[5] Judges 6:12, emphasis added.

I hope you will read Gideon's story to see how preposterous that label must have sounded to him. He was in hiding when he received that message. But God could see the valiant warrior Gideon would prove to be when, following God in obedience, he led Israel to victory.

I like to look at Gideon from a running back's perspective. Previously, I described how an NFL running back has to run to where the hole is designed to be, even before he sees the hole open; because if he waits for the hole to open, it will close again before he can run through it. That's often called *vision* for a back.

For me, the first part of vision in the NFL was understanding the play's design. I had to spend time studying the playbook to know where the hole would be. Then I had to trust my offensive linemen to open that hole. But I also had to time it right, because if I got to that spot too soon, I would run into the back of a blocker; and if I arrived too late, the hole would be gone. Trust and timing were essential.

Vision extended beyond the line of scrimmage. When I ran the ball, I didn't look at the defensive linemen. Instead, I looked beyond them to the second and third levels to anticipate what the linebackers and secondary would do. If I saw the defense flowing quickly in one direction, I would look for where I could cut back behind their flow. On many zone plays, I cut back all the way across the field after passing through the first level. I had numerous conversations with receivers about hustling and blocking on the backside because of the likelihood I would cut back and run their way. That level of vision was how we produced so many long run plays.

In running back terms, Gideon was waiting for the hole to open up, and God was telling him to run to where He would open the hole for him. When Gideon finally trusted God and moved in that direction—when he became a moving target—God worked through him to defeat Israel's enemies. Gideon's trust in God opened the way for a significant victory for all of Israel.

A lot of people believe *in* God, but far fewer believe God. They don't place their trust in Him.

I encourage you to believe Him and to trust in Him. Spend time studying the playbook—the Bible—to better understand Him. Take a step of faith and become a moving target. God will open doors for you where you did not know doors existed, because He designed those doors for you to go through. And when an opportunity presents itself, ask, "What is the Lord calling me to do?" Here's a hint: The answer will involve other people, because your purpose is never solely about you. Purpose is always about others.

Everything I've mentioned in this epilogue begins with seeking Christ. Look at that word: *seeking*. We can break it down like this: *see-king*. See the King.

To quote Matthew 6:33 again: "Seek first the kingdom of God and his righteousness, and all these things will be provided for you."

I teach my children, "Seek first the kingdom of God and His righteousness, and then it's plainly written out for you—all these other things will be added to you." Within those other things is exactly what you need to serve God, because He knows exactly what you need.

Seek Jesus first, last, and in between, because He is the only one worth seeking.

It's not about you.

It's *all* about Him.

Acknowledgments

Danielle

I want to acknowledge the strength, perseverance, and virtue you possess, which I can sometimes take for granted or overlook. I recognize how rare it is for someone to embody all three. Being loved by you has produced incomparable growth in me and has had a profound, positive impact on my life. Thank you for being my best friend and ALWAYS for me!

> Charm is deceptive and beauty is fleeting,
> but a woman who fears the Lord will be praised.
>
> PROVERBS 31:30

Mom and Dad

These heartfelt words of acknowledgment don't even scratch the surface of rightly honoring the great sacrifice you both made in raising two rambunctious boys in southern Louisiana. I sometimes feel guilty that I was given such great parents, because that's surely not everyone's experience; but ultimately I'm overcome with gratitude. God's grace transcends generations, and He has absolutely lavished His love and grace on me with y'all.

> A good man leaves an inheritance to his grandchildren,
> but the sinner's wealth is stored up for the righteous.
>
> PROVERBS 13:22

About the Authors

Matt Forté was drafted by the Chicago Bears in the second round of the 2008 NFL draft. His rookie season ranks among the most prolific in franchise history, and he was one of the league's best dual-threat backs during his eight seasons with the Bears. During his ten years in the league, the two-time Pro Bowler amassed 14,468 total yards and scored 75 touchdowns. In 2014, Matt set a single-season NFL record for running backs, with 102 receptions.

On April 23, 2018, Matt signed a one-day contract and officially retired as a Chicago Bear. He remains one of five running backs in NFL history to record 100 or more receptions in a single season and one of four to amass 100 or more receptions and 1,000+ rushing yards in a single season. In August 2023, he was inducted into the Louisiana Sports Hall of Fame, recognized for his athletic contributions as a Louisiana native and graduate of Tulane University.

After his retirement, Matt developed an athleisure clothing brand called Workhorse 22 Apparel. He also hosts the *Sports Spectrum* podcast, works with his wife, Danielle, as a codirector of marriage ministry for Pro Athletes Outreach, and continues to develop his What's Your Forté Foundation. The foundation, started in 2013, guides youths (especially in disinvested areas) toward becoming their best selves, providing specific resources and access to career paths that accentuate their talents and potential so they can realize their purpose in life. Young people are inspired to pursue a calling, instead of just a job, which in turn helps fight against society's main plagues of violence, fatherlessness, and poverty.

David L. Thomas is the author/cowriter of more than twenty books, including *New York Times* bestsellers *Foxcatcher* and *Wrestling for My Life*. He previously worked for almost three decades in sports journalism. David and his wife, Sally, live near Fort Worth, Texas, and have two grown children and one grandchild. He can be reached through his website, davidthomasauthor.com.